ÉTIENNE GARBUGLI

Find Your Market

Discover And Win Your Product's Best Market Opportunity

First edition

ISBN: 978-1-7771604-8-7

Proofreading by Joy Sellen
Cover art by Katarina Naskovski

This book was professionally typeset on Reedsy.
Find out more at reedsy.com

To the entrepreneurs and innovators willing to take the risk of bringing new products to market.

Contents

III New Markets

How to Use This Book

The approach in *Find Your Market* was designed to be modular.

Not only is the book *intentionally* short—you're trying to make progress, not read books—it can be broken down into different paths, each tailored to the specific needs of the situation you find yourself in.

In the first section, **Getting Started**, you will gain a better understanding of the situation your team is in. If your product currently has users or customers, you'll be able to evaluate whether a segment of that audience could become the gateway to a broader market.

If you don't currently have customers or a user base—or if you don't think any of your customers could open market opportunities—the next section, **New Markets**, will help you flesh out the core value of your innovation, brainstorm markets worth exploring, and strategically evaluate the most promising opportunities.

Once you have identified a few markets that could be worth pursuing, **Validating Your Findings** will help you gain conclusive evidence that a market you're exploring is actually worth committing to (or alternatively, should be cast aside).

Once a market has been validated, the last section, **Speed**, will help you mold your positioning and go-to-market strategy to the segments that your team has chosen to focus on.

Throughout the book, you'll find markers (▸▸) indicating opportunities to jump ahead to more appropriate content, or suggestions to revisit specific exercises in the previous sections (◂◂). These markers, and the content under **Troubleshooting**, were designed to help ensure that you're making real progress commercializing your innovation.

I really hope you enjoy *Find Your Market*—it's a book I really enjoyed writing.

I

Introduction

1

Why this Book

"Everybody has a strategy until they get handed a big check.[1]" – Karen Peacock, Intercom CEO

When I was a kid, I wanted to be an inventor.

I'd spend hours in my room dreaming up inventions.

Sometimes these inventions became rough products made from discarded parts (read: trash), sometimes they'd turn into LEGO block constructions, but most times they stayed as drawings.

I'd sometimes revisit those drawings to improve my *designs*, somehow convincing myself that adding details would bring these inventions one step closer to reality.

As I gained experience and the products I built evolved from LEGO bricks, to early websites, to fully-functioning technology products, two things became clear:

1. Innovation is a lot harder than it looks.

2. There's a massive chasm between an idea and its adoption as a viable solution by real customers.

Sometimes things click. You have the right idea at the right time and you're able to share it with the right audience, simply.

Most times, however, the path from idea to commercialization and scale is a lot murkier.

There are countless examples of great technologies, ideas, or inventions that failed to gain traction.

However, if we take a deep look at many of the innovations that have failed to be adopted, we can see a clear pattern...

Technology. Problems.

According to CB Insights' list of the top reasons why startups fail[2] (or any similar studies really[3]), the main reason why startups fail is: 'no market need'.

Although there's value in similar simplifications, this reason should really read as 'no market need *found before the team ran out of money and/or motivation*'.

As you'll see throughout this book, given enough time, money, and willingness to iterate, any viable technology can ultimately find its use.

It was true with my first startup, Flagback, whose main competitors[4] are still profitable and growing. It was true with my second startup, HireVoice, which could have become Officevibe or any of its numerous competitors[5]. It was also true with my third startup, Highlights[6], which got acquired, but now faces much tougher competition[7].

At its core, technology solves problems. In general, the bigger the problems, and the more efficiently those problems are solved, then the bigger the payoff is for innovators.

When your starting point is a product—or you have strong technological innovation—you're going backwards, trying to match a breakthrough to a market, pain point, use case, or Job to be Done.

This, is often viewed as *having a solution looking for a problem.* It's a challenge that tends to require a different approach to customer development...

The Challenge With Customer Development

I wrote my first book, Lean B2B, the way an inventor would: I wanted to solve my own problem, to find the most efficient way to get from idea to product/market fit (PMF) in B2B.

Through many iterations, Lean B2B became a book that could help entrepreneurs find early adopters, identify and prioritize business opportunities, convince business stakeholders to share pain points, create a minimum viable product, and iterate until they're able to find PMF.

Thankfully, I wasn't the only one facing these challenges. As the book grew in popularity, the content got introduced to accelerators, consultants, intrapreneurs, universities, and government agencies.

Now the book is used by startups, governments, consultants, large companies, students, and other interest groups outside the audience that I originally planned to serve.

This has created challenges. Many entrepreneurs—or other types of innovators—don't get to start their innovation process with a blank slate. They either start with a technology, an idea, or business requirements, or they have parts of a working product that they try to get growing. Adapting the Lean B2B methodology to these situations forces a certain leap, and as I've seen with many entrepreneurs, leaps introduce new risks.

Deciding which market opportunity to focus on is a major decision that can significantly impact the success potential of a new venture. It's my strong belief that by clarifying the process of finding the right market for an innovation, the survival rate of new enterprises will increase significantly.

The Market of Find Your Market

Much like books, technology products can provide value to different audiences.

The more *generalized* or general-purpose a technology is, the more distinct market opportunities there usually can be:

Domain-specific   **Generalized**

Figure 1.1 – The number of market opportunities for domain-specific and generalized innovations

And the more generally applicable a product or technology is, the greater the dilemma innovators are faced with. The same innovation may be valuable to dozens of different types of users or organizations. The technology might be the same, but the upside may be radically different. *How do you know which opportunity you should focus on?*

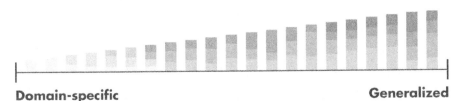

Domain-specific   **Generalized**

Figure 1.2 – The market potential for domain-specific and generalized innovations

Although *Find Your Market* will help both types of entrepreneurs find a market for their innovation, it was specially designed to meet the needs of the innovators who are struggling to pick the right market when the options are varied, and the upside can vary greatly.

This might include:

1. **Startups**: Startup founders may have already built a full product, or large parts of a product, that they're hoping to bring to market—or they may wish to test many markets before deciding to make a commitment. They may be hoping to commercialize technology that requires significant upfront innovation, as is often the case with deep tech startups. *Find Your Market* will help startups to clarify the unique value of their technology, shortlist its most promising applications, and ultimately, point out their best path forward.

2. **Technology-push firms**: Technology-push organizations like Technology Transfer Offices (TTOs) or Research Commercialization Offices are tasked with the direct commercialization of inventions and research findings, or with their indirect commercialization through partnerships. In *Find Your Market* these organizations will discover a clear system for assessing the commercial viability of their innovations. Should they decide to bring those innovations to market themselves, the book will also give them a framework to help structure their go-to-market strategy.

3. **Mid- to large-size organizations**: Businesses (ranging from agencies to

large product organizations) may have developed unique technologies or expertise that they hope to either *productize* or bring to market. Whether this is through technology spin-offs or ongoing research into new applications of their technologies, such teams will benefit from having clear processes to facilitate effective market selection decisions.

No matter the situation you find yourself in, *Find Your Market* will meet you where you are, and help you progress. But to be able to make progress, you need to understand where you're starting from. In the next chapter, we'll make a first assessment.

II

Getting Started

In this section, you'll gain a better understanding of the situation you find yourself in. If you have users or customers, you can learn whether a segment of that audience might point to significant opportunities for your product.

2

The Starting Point

""Move fast and break things" sounds good until you realize you're moving in the wrong direction and everything's broken.[8] " – Danny Trinh, Zenly Head of Design

Innovation ideas can come from anywhere.

They may be the result of a careful analysis of consumer behaviors, or a hunch based on disruptions in the technological landscape, or the result of a eureka moment.

Unfortunately, great ideas don't always come with a blueprint of who the user or customer should be. In fact, sometimes disregarding user or customer needs is what makes the technological breakthrough possible in the first place[9].

No matter what the reason, new products are launched all the time without having clear and validated customer segments. Sometimes these products quickly find their aim, but sometimes they struggle to find their first customers, let alone their first users.

When innovations meet the market, everything gets bundled up—prospects make split-second decisions based on a mashup of the company name, design, copy, value proposition, their understanding of what the technology enables, imagined comparables, social proof, and price point. And all this often happens *before* prospects even engage with the product, or connect with its sales team.

It becomes extremely difficult to untangle the results. *Was the product wrong? Did the right folks show up? Were we targeting the right market? Was the value proposition clear? Can we conclude anything from our launch?!*

To be able to make progress, you need clarity. And when everything's tangled up—and your product isn't getting a ton of use, leads, or visits—it's hard to know what direction to take.

When Plans Meet Reality

Maybe your product's initial launch was a year ago. Or maybe it was just a few weeks back.

Chances are that it looked something like this:

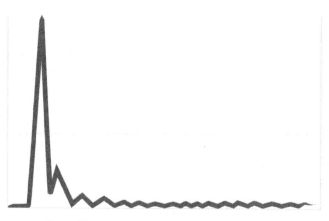

Figure 2.1 – Sample traffic surrounding the launch of a new technology product

Initially, things were probably extremely busy. Lots of traffic. Lots of use. Messages coming in. Everything was really exciting, but then the excitement tailed off, and while some users signed on, others moved on.

Over time, more users came, and left again. As you're reading this, you may be left with:

- a disparate group of customers using your product for different reasons;
- users coming in and out with spotty usage patterns;
- various types of data, feedback, and support messaging pulling your team in different directions;
- some successes and failures; *and*
- more confusion than clarity.

It's hard to know what the best path is when everything is lumped together.

▸▸

```
If you haven't launched, or if you don't currently have users or
customers, feel free to jump ahead to Chapter #5, What a Great
Market Looks Like.
```

Launches Are Rarely 1 or 0

Too often, when innovators launch new products based on a technological breakthrough, they try to keep their targeting broad. Because they're not entirely sure who they're trying to sell to, they avoid over-committing one way or another.

As a result, the positioning of their product often feels like a caricature of reality—the value proposition is bland, the messaging is broad and untargeted, and the pain points sound hollow, sometimes imagined.

When users sign up, or when they buy, they do it based on what they understand, or what they can infer while using the product. This might mean that the product attracts audiences that are completely different from those that were initially intended, or that people of the exact right profile don't even realize that the product was made for them.

Similar mismatches are a regular occurrence in the early days of startups. Just as *your* perception of the value of your innovation can be different from the market's perception, your users and site visitors may be seeing something completely different in your product.

In fact, early adopters—the people who are willing to sign on to get certain competitive advantages or benefits before the rest of the market gets them—may be using your product with the aim of gaining benefits that your team might not have set out to enable.

Zooming in, digging in, and understanding the various patterns of use might reveal significant market opportunities.

There might be users who, if you were to wholly mold your product to their needs, could open up opportunities. After all, as *From Impossible to Inevitable* co-authors Jason M. Lemkin and Aaron Ross say[10]: *"If you have one customer in an industry, you can get 10. The outliers aren't anomalies, they are the future."* The real question is: *should you?*

Taking Stock of Your User Base

When your product has usage, it makes sense to start by unpacking the value that your users and customers see (or fail to see) in your product.

This might reveal needs, segments, and markets that you haven't considered—or it could make you decide to move on and explore new markets for your innovation.

This analysis is often the shortest path to finding a great market opportunity.

In the next chapter we'll see how.

3

Mining for Gold

"Feedback is just noise until you segment it.[11]*"* – Des Traynor,
Intercom Co-Founder

By the end of this chapter, your users and customers—whether you have one
or a thousand—should fit on a map like the following:

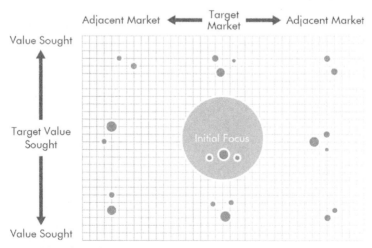

*Figure 3.1 – Mapping of a user or customer base around their market groupings
and the value sought*

They will be from different markets, they will have sought different value from your product, and they will have got different results out of it.

Some combinations of markets and value will generate great results, others won't. If your team dedicates itself to growing them, some of these combinations could turn into fast-growing businesses, while others might destroy your business completely.

The more users and customers you have had, and the fuzzier or more ineffective your messaging has been, the more value/market combinations you're likely to discover.

To get a sense of the opportunity set, and ultimately to be able to make good decisions, you need to surface as many of these combinations as possible.

Now, since you probably don't have a clear idea of who has been using your product and why, you need to start with what you *can* know: the outcomes.

Analyzing the Outcomes

You may not know exactly *why* users and customers have behaved the way they did, but you *can* tell what has happened.

At this stage, there are ways for you to know which users have found the most value with your product, and which users have generated the most value for your company.

This information, in turn, will allow you to rank your users from best to worst:

Figure 3.2 – Force-ranked user base

On one side, you'll have your absolute best customers, your "fans" or advocates. On the other, will be your least valuable users and customers, those that probably *shouldn't* have been targeted.

By comparing great, good, and bad fits, you can find the attributes that influence whether or not a customer relationship will work out.

For example, if you realize that many of your top-performing users work for large organizations, and that many of your worst users are consumers or freelancers, you might assume that business size—or the simple fact that they work for businesses—is a key criterion.

Since the idea of what a great customer is depends largely on the type of product and business that you're building, you will have to come up with your own unique way—your recipe—to identify your best users.

Typically, this recipe will be a mix of:

1. **Revenue**: Customer lifetime value (CLV)—how much revenue is generated over the entire duration of the customer relationship—is often a good way to find your highest spending customers.
2. **Engagement/Retention/Value**: A good way to evaluate engagement might be how often core product actions are performed, or by looking at 7-, 14-, or 28-day retention rates. If there is a metric that can help you

get a sense of the value that the user has been able to extract from your product, then this metric might be even better.

3. **Referral/Word of Mouth**: For word of mouth, this might be the number of referrals sent or completed, or a Net Promoter Score (NPS)®. Atlassian is an example of a company that uses customer NPS to find segments that are worth growing[12].

Your recipe may also include factors that are more specific to your business model. Feel free to browse the list of factors in Chapter #8 for inspiration.

The larger your user base is, the more criteria you can include in your segmentation without drying the pool too much.

Don't take this too far. Simply look for an effective way to force-rank your users and customers:

#	NAME	REVENUE	ENGAGEMENT	REFERRALS	TOTAL
1	Isabella Guertin	10	7	3	20
2	Mason Marek	7	8	4	19
3	Mónica María Gutiérrez	6	5	6	17
4	Mike Amber	5	8	3	16
5	Robert Friedman	4	6	4	14
...	...				

Figure 3.3 – Example of a user or customer list, ranked

Experiment with your recipe to make sure that you're not missing out on great users. With each change, look at the profiles (and their behaviors) that are coming up on top and at the bottom. *Are those the people that you'd expect to find there?*

Depending on how technical you are, you may be able to create your ranking using SQL, a CRM, database exports, or by looking at people analytics in tools like Amplitude, Mixpanel, or Intercom.

Recruiting for User Interviews

Once your user base is ranked, you should start recruiting for interviews.

Each interview should take roughly 20–30 minutes. With this series of interviews, your goal is to discover and explore the various value/market combinations in your user base.

Each interview will allow you to learn about the type of value that users were seeking, why they were looking for these specific benefits, and what happened once they began interacting with your product.

These interviews will give you ample opportunities to unpack your interviewees' (mis)understanding. You may realize that a group of users was seeking an altogether different solution, or that they simply didn't understand that your product could deliver the value that they were looking for.

You can short-cut your learning process by comparing the information that they share with their actual use and interactions with your product.

To start recruiting, focus on users that are either still active, or that have stopped using your product within the last 90 days. Beyond that, their recollection of facts and events might be blurry. You should also make sure that they were given enough time to try and use your product, whether they did, or they didn't.

Although the ideal situation would be to speak to *all* of your users to discover every single value/market variation, in reality, this usually isn't possible.

Look at your rankings, and randomly recruit a sample of 12–15 participants from your top 20–30% users. A sample of this size will help balance depth and coverage.

You should also recruit the same number of participants from the bottom 70–80%. This second grouping will help you contrast the information captured, and may point to instances where users were looking for the value that your product is able to deliver, but got confused by your messaging.

As you'll see in the Informavores case study later, the best opportunities aren't always the most common.

Considering that you'll likely need to contact five times more users than the number of interviews that you're trying to land, your user base needs to be of a certain size. If you don't have enough users or customers to recruit from, simply make sure that your recruitment is balanced between groups, and that you're speaking to at least 12–15 users in total.

You can use the battle-tested message at findyourmarket.co/invite to invite users and customers for interviews, or you can craft your own.

Conducting Interviews

Interviews help you understand which market groupings your interviewees fall into, as well as the specific value that they were seeking.

The best way to get to this type of information is through Switch interviews—the most effective interview type for understanding decision-making processes that lead up to using, or trying a product.

These interviews focus on capturing the story of a user's relationship with a product from *First-Thought* (when they first began looking for the value of the product), through to *First Use*, and all the way to *On-Going Usage* or *Disengagement*:

Figure 3.4 – The Switch timeline (also known as the JTBD timeline)

They allow you to understand why users or customers 'hired'—or were hoping to 'hire'—your product. *What Job are they trying to get Done?*

To capture useful information, you should begin by asking the participant to share, in detail, the circumstances that led them to your product. Then, you need to follow their story chronologically along the Switch timeline.

Asking detailed, specific questions about tangible aspects is a good way to jog an interviewee's memory.

Here's what your question list could look like:

- *How did you first hear about [Product] ? What did you know about it at the time?*
- *What was going on in your life at that time?*

- *Did you imagine what life would be like with the product? What were you expecting?*
- *What was your previous experience with [Solution Space]?*
- *What was wrong with what you were using?*
- *What made you decide to [Buy / Use] the product?*
- *Did you evaluate other products?*
- *Did anyone else weigh in on the decision?*
- *What was the main thing that convinced you?*
- *Once you [Signed up / Bought], how did the product compare to your expectations?*
- *What surprised you (good or bad)? Why did it surprise you?*
- *Now that you have [Product] what can you do that you couldn't do before?*
- *What is the main value you feel you've received from the product?*
- *What is the main problem you feel that the product solves for you?*
- *Why do you keep using the product?*
- *If we took away [Product] from you, what would be the things you miss most? What would you use as an alternative?*
- *Now that you're using [Product], who would you recommend it to and why?*

Don't jump to conclusions too quickly. At this stage, you're just trying to explore and discover the value/market combinations.

Consider recording these discussions and then sharing the raw files with teammates who aren't involved in the interview process. This will help them make their own conclusions, and will increase the overall objectivity of your analysis.

Put some time between finalizing the interviews and analyzing the data. We'll start breaking things down in the next chapter.

Case Study :: How Informavores Doubled its Growth Rate by Zooming in on a 20% Use Case

Informavores was founded in 2004 by Steve Wood in Cardiff, Wales. The original idea for the product was to allow users to draw flow diagrams, which could then be converted into fully functioning software applications.

Although the vision was big and the idea was simple, the market proved to be really challenging.

After one year building the first version of the product, and another one trying to sell the software with few successes to show for, it was clear that each customer had very different needs.

With so many differences, it was hard to grow the company in a standardized way.

The company was failing. Steve was slowly going bankrupt. Until, one day, through what ended up being a heated discussion[13], a consultant from PricewaterhouseCoopers made Steve realize that Informavores was a good business—but they weren't trying to grow it nearly hard enough.

Following this conversation, Steve got to work creating a new plan for the company. He wanted to refocus Informavores around a single vertical with a single use case. Instead of selling a generalized platform that could do different things for different people, they would solve one major pain for one market.

Having done a lot of the sales himself, Steve had a hunch that the company should refocus on call guidance workflows for contact centers, a use case that at the time only accounted for 20% of their revenue.

It was a gut decision. The team wasn't happy with the much smaller vision, but it didn't take long for this new direction to show promise.

Within 12 months, Informavores had signed deals with the US Department of Defense, Microsoft, Symantec, HP, and many more large organizations.

Their growth rate had more than doubled. By focusing on a single use case, they were able to find a reliable growth engine, specialize their backlog, and address customer problems with more depth than before.

In 2009, the company was acquired by Salesforce. Informavores would go on to become one of the backbones of the Salesforce Platform (ex-Force.com).

Looking back, Steve says that the challenge really boiled down to 1) figuring out who the customer was and why they were buying, and 2) finding a way to reach them.

Sometimes the answers are hidden in plain sight. Informavores found success when they doubled down on a use case that a segment of their customers was already paying for.

Taking Action (5-10 days)

1. Think about what a great user or customer of your product would look like.
2. Use this definition (recipe) to rank your users from best to worst.
3. Randomly recruit participants in two key groupings.
4. Conduct 20–minute Switch interviews and learn.

4

Can It Be a Market?

"There may be a gap in the market, but is there a market in the gap?"

What did the interviews reveal? Did some users or customers seem particularly engaged or interested? Did you discover promising use cases?

Go back to the chart that we were planning to fill at the end of the previous chapter. On the vertical axis, list the different value that interviewees were hoping to get from your product.

Use size, or a different color, to indicate your most valuable users or customers:

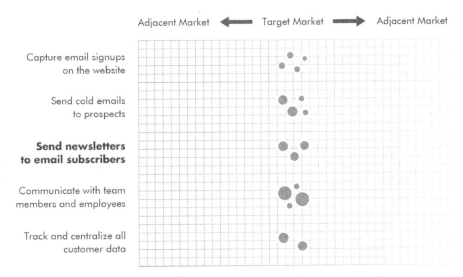

Figure 4.1 – Example of the mapping of a user or customer base

At a glance, the map should help summarize both the type of value that your users were seeking, and how they behaved.

The best opportunities will come from two groups on your chart:

1. **Right-fits**: Users or customers who were attempting to use your product for its core value. For these users, you should focus on whether or not they were able to find success, if they were able to understand that your product delivers the value that they were seeking, and why they ended up becoming disengaged (if they did).
2. **Unexpected successes**: Users or customers who were looking for benefits other than those intended, or who were hoping to solve another problem—but were still able to find success with your product. For these users, you need to figure out what problem your product solves for them, and the type of value that they feel your product delivers.

We'll extract market opportunities by digging into the profiles and behaviors of users and customers in these two groups.

27

Extrapolating Markets

In essence, a market is a set of potential customers who share a pain, problem, need, or Job to be Done that will reference each other's purchase decision for a specific need.

At any moment, the same person may be part of one, or several markets. For example, there might be little to no overlap in my membership in the markets of:

- People who work in pharma (industry);
- People who work in sales (function);
- People whose income taxes are late (problem);
- People that listen to music (Job);
- People who play chess (hobby);
- People who are learning to invest in crypto (opportunity).

Much like me, your interviewees will be part of multiple markets.

Although they might fit in many markets, there will generally be one affiliation or market that *causes* them to seek the value of your product.

For example, I wrote this book using a tool called Reedsy[14]. The reason why I used this tool is not because I'm part of the chess playing market (I'm not), it's because I'm part of the market of people who write books (authors).

Get back to your interview data. For each user or customer in your *right-fit* and *unexpected success* groupings, ask:

*What affiliation **caused** this person to seek out our product?*

And update the previous chart with the new information:

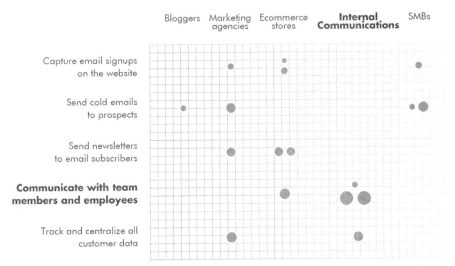

Figure 4.2 – Example of the mapping of a user or customer base with market groupings

Are there groupings that repeat? Are there surprising groupings? Which groupings seem most promising?

In the above example, the most promising opportunity might be internal communication teams using the product to communicate with team members and employees.

Take note of the most interesting market groupings and keep moving.

Is There a Market in The Gap?

It's easy to get excited by the opportunities that you discover. You may find one or several great use cases that could open up market opportunities. And you could simply jump in, adjust your product's functionalities, and start going all in—the way Informavores did. At this stage, however, the cost of making rash decisions can be tremendous. Before going all in, you should do your research.

For a grouping to make sense, there must be channels where prospects can exchange and share purchase decisions. Without these, it will be difficult for your business to grow fast.

Markets generally self-organize around communities and watering holes. To confirm that your groupings can lead to real markets, you'll want to find those watering holes.

Perform searches around your market groupings. For example: "[Market] + mailing list", "[Market] + forum"; "[Market] + competition", or other keywords including Twitter, group, list, community, help, wiki, questions, meetup, list, resources, association, customers, tutorials, awards, user group, or blog.

You could also use a tool like The Hive Index[15] to find communities in the market.

If there are active watering holes where prospects exchange and share purchase decisions, then you're probably dealing with a real market.

For each grouping that you consider, also ask:

- **Is this a market of one?** *Can you point to other customers like the one(s) that you identified? How are they connected? How would they be able to share their purchase decisions? Would there be enough customers to sustain your business?*
- **Could you reach them?** *Are there channels that you can use to reach similar prospects? How responsive would they be?*
- **Do you have the right product?** *How different are their needs from what you're already offering? If you make product enhancements to meet their needs, would those changes align with your vision for the company?*
- **Could you help them get return on their investment (ROI)?** *Could customers achieve the success they seek? Will this provide significantly more value than*

the alternatives? Can this be done predictably and repeatably?

- **Is there urgency?** Pain is one of the best predictors of future behaviors. *How likely is it that customers decide to do nothing? Is there enough momentum for them to want to make a change? What would their core reason to act be?*
- **Do prospects have money?** *Do they currently have budget? Do they have the authority to make their own purchases? Can they easily access funds to buy?*
- **Would this market fit your overall strategy?** *Would you be locked in in this market? Would winning this market help you achieve your strategic goals? Could it help you expand into other markets?*
- **If made successful, could customers provide references freely?** Some industries are *opaque*, effectively limiting word of mouth. *Could customers recommend your product freely? Are there other prospects in their networks?* It's important for customer references to attract the right people.
- **Would you like to work with them?** *Would you be happy selling and networking in this market? Does it make sense for you long term?*

Although few markets will meet all criteria, this type of evaluation process will at least ensure that your decision is well thought out.

Going All In

You've identified a market that looks promising. It ticks most of the boxes. *Time to go all in?*

It's difficult to commit to a market when you don't know what other opportunities may be available. If your company's timeline and financial situation permits, it can be a really good idea to spend the next month exploring a broader set of markets in *Part III*. Your search might point to a better opportunity for your innovation, or it might confirm that the opportunity that you have identified in this section is the best one for you.

If, however, you're short on time or if you have a strong belief that the market identified here will work itself out, feel free to jump to *Part IV* to start validating the market.

Deciding which market to focus on is an important decision that shouldn't be rushed. Research has shown that carefully evaluating many market opportunities has a positive impact on the odds of success for new ventures[16]. Ultimately, spending a little more time evaluating markets can really pay off for your team.

▸▸

If you feel like the market opportunity that you identified could be interesting for your product, consider jumping ahead to Chapter #12, Validating Markets. If not, keep reading.

Taking Action (2 hours)

1. List the value that interviewees were hoping to get from your product. Identify your most valuable users and customers.
2. Extrapolate the market groupings that *caused* users to seek out your product's value.
3. Validate that your market groupings actually act like markets.
4. Use the checklist in this chapter to evaluate the remaining market opportunities.
5. Make an informed decision.

III

New Markets

In this main section of Find Your Market, you will learn what a market is, and what it isn't. You'll also be shown how to flesh out the core value of your innovation, identify markets that are worth exploring, and gather data on your most promising market opportunities.

5

What a Great Market Looks Like

"There is only one winning strategy. It is to carefully define the target market and direct a superior offering to that target market." – Philip Kotler, Marketing Management Author

Veeva Systems was founded by Peter Gassner and Matt Wallach in 2007.

Having seen the evolution of client-server and mainframe technologies earlier in their careers, the founders believed that, as the cloud matured, products would become more verticalized, targeting specific industry segments[17].

At Salesforce, where he spent four years working as VP of Technology, Gassner had identified an opportunity to create a CRM for the life science industry. The Force.com platform, which he had helped build, could help them get to market fast.

He teamed up with Wallach—a life science veteran who understood the customer needs and what these companies valued in technology, and had a sense of which organizations might become early adopters—and they were off to the races.

Although this might read like a great start point today, at the time, the Force platform was unproven, the life sciences industry was highly regulated (it still is), and the cloud was still nascent.

Friends and investors were cautioning them, telling them that their market would be too small, and that they wouldn't be able to exit.

Yet, the idea of building a CRM addressing the specific needs of the life science industry on the Salesforce platform turned out to be a stroke of genius.

Not only were they able to demonstrate that they could handle the security requirements of the industry, they proved that their CRM would get used by the industry's sales professionals[18].

Within a few years, Veeva signed many large clients, including Novartis, Pfizer, and Johnson & Johnson.

In 2010, the company launched a second verticalized product, Veeva Vault, designed to help large and small life science organizations manage their content and data.

Through strategic acquisitions and the development of new functionalities, Veeva became the platform of choice for the industry.

Today, with a market cap of over $40 billion built off a strong IPO in 2013, Veeva has shown that their market was never really *too small*; it had just never been addressed specifically enough.

Why Veeva Systems Won

So, *what made Veeva a success?*

When Wallach and Gassner made the decision to start their business, CRMs had been around for almost 40 years, the life science industry was well established, enterprise software was well understood, and cloud CRM was becoming big business[19].

Yet, in spite of all this, Gassner recounts[20] that before starting the company, one of his friends made a drawing on a paper napkin, hoping to make him understand: *"Here's enterprise software. Now, here's life sciences. That's a very small wedge. Here's pharma CRM. That's like a pin prick."*

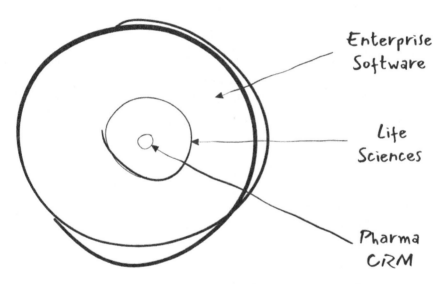

Figure 5.1 – Illustration of Veeva's market opportunity

Veeva was ultimately able to prove that if a market vertical is large enough, and the company is able to continuously expand its relationship with customers, it can lead to a massive opportunity.

Although the founders probably didn't expect Veeva to become a $40 billion company, or that they would remain solely focused on the needs of the life science industry, Gassner's experiences working for a large horizontal cloud CRM vendor like Salesforce had made him realize that life sciences had the potential to be a lucrative vertical, and that it had a very distinct viewpoint.

Not only did life science sales staff have different needs, they faced higher levels of regulations, they worked on different timelines, had different jargon, and were involved in different events and communities. In many ways, the life sciences industry was its own universe, created by regulations and the unique nature of the work.

Early on, the founders had to overcome access, regulatory, and credibility challenges, but by building on top of a proven platform like Salesforce's, leveraging Wallach's connections, and staying laser-focused on the customer needs, they were able to take the market by storm.

Their arrival allowed life science sales staff—who were probably dissatisfied with the gaps in their horizontal CRMs—to finally get a product that could address their full needs.

The more life science organizations bought from them, the better they were able to understand and address the customer requirements. The more credibility they gained, the more deeply entrenched in the market they became.

What a Market Really Is

Veeva may very well have been the biggest vertical software success story in history.

Although the founders targeted one of the richest verticals (bringing a new drug to market costs around $1.3 billion[21]), their story helps to illustrate what a good market is.

Great markets, like life sciences, have some sort of fencing around them. There's a sense of identity and belonging. For example, someone might say

*"I work in **life sciences**", or "I'm a **chemist** and I work in **life sciences**."*

As a result of that identity, or that shared experience, these markets have their own watering holes (blogs, conferences, forums, mailing lists, etc) where prospects gather to learn, exchange, and connect. They also have their own leadership (experts, influencers, personalities, speakers, etc), their own jargon, and sometimes their own beliefs and worldviews.

You can think of great markets as select clubs. If well-positioned, products can become a part of their market's identity. For example, today, many sales people will actually refuse to work for organizations that use another CRM than Salesforce[22]. *This* can effectively create a powerful competitive advantage for the company.

In a lot of ways, large markets are groupings of smaller markets. At any moment, a person can be part of one, or several markets:

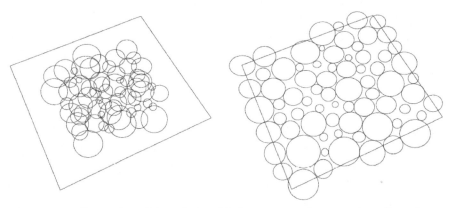

Figure 5.2 – Illustration of the relationship between market groupings (based on a diagram by researcher Valdis Krebs)

There are many ways to group individuals or companies into markets. For example, the markets you'll explore or identify might ultimately be based on:

- roles like designers (e.g. Figma) or developers (e.g. Github);
- functions like sales (e.g. Salesforce) or human resources (e.g. Workday);
- industries like Oil & Gas (e.g. Flutura in Chapter #14);
- verticals like life sciences (e.g. Veeva Systems);
- hobbies like model construction (e.g. LEGO) or motorcycle driving (e.g. Harley Davidson);
- problems or Jobs to be Done like transferring money (e.g. PayPal), listening to music (e.g. Spotify), or keeping marketing and sales data in sync (e.g. Outfunnel);
- worldviews like *simple software is better* (e.g. Basecamp); or
- any other attribute(s) that can create a sense of belonging.

To avoid wasting a lot of time, people within your target market must either *already* view themselves as part of a market, or you must be able to bring them together into a market of your own definition (i.e. create the category).

A fragmented market—or many small markets that aren't related—will never create a big market. Although the exact market groupings for your innovation will become clearer once you start interacting with prospects, for now, it's important to understand how a market's size will impact your ability to take an innovation to market.

Finding the Right Fit (And the Right Size)

PayPal didn't start by trying to capture the entire online money transfer market. No. They got their first break when they started targeting eBay PowerSellers[23].

Their vision was huge—allowing anyone to email money—but early on, they had to work with a tiny segment of users with niche use cases to get the engines going.

At the time, eBay sellers had to wait weeks for checks to arrive by mail, and then sometimes also weeks for the money to clear. For PowerSellers, there were huge benefits to getting paid through PayPal. Yet, today, PowerSellers probably don't even register in eBay's financial reports.

Entrepreneurs tend to think of markets in terms of the Total Addressable Market (TAM)—the revenue potential of the entire market that they intend to pursue. Because they are trying to drum up interest from investors, create a business plan, or simply impress, they'll try to make their market as big as possible.

The resulting market might include several verticals, niches, or industries. Their TAM may be massive, but when comes time to establish an initial foothold in the market, they won't know what to do.

The truth is that, most of the concepts used to explain the scale of markets—TAMs, SAMs[24], or SOMs[25]—aren't very useful when entrepreneurs are trying to get the engines going, and survival is on the line.

Early on, you don't want to make your market bigger, you want to make it *smaller*.

A better concept early on is what investor Michael Skok calls the Minimum Viable Segment (MVS)[26].

A MVS is a segment of a market that exhibits the same, or similar needs, or that seeks the same value in the same way. It's generally a segment that is *selected* from a market.

For example, while exploring the Medical Device market, you might realize that a sub-segment of the Critical Care market has very similar needs. After careful consideration, you might decide to make this grouping your MVS. The point of emphasis here is that this is a decision that *you*, the innovator, make.

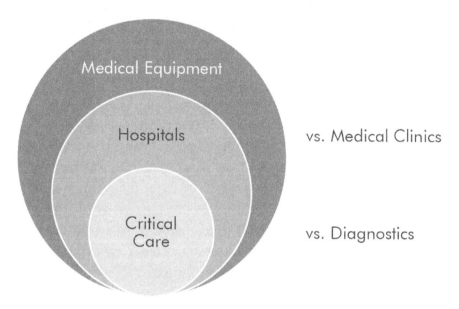

Figure 5.3 – Example of an MVS carved out of a larger market

A good MVS is small enough to be actionable, it's part of a broader market in which you can eventually expand, and it can be dominated to help establish a beachhead and gain a leadership position in a relatively short time frame.

To avoid building a product for a market of one, a MVS needs to be comprised of many prospects. However, the actual size of the segment really depends on your revenue requirements.

A good rule of thumb with entry markets is that they should be large enough to sustain your company.

Your MVS will simply be your entry point. Once you have found a good opportunity, you'll want to zoom out to capture adjacent segments of the market. But to get anywhere, first you need to find a segment that you can act on.

Taking Action (1 hour)

1. Familiarize yourself with the attributes of a good market.
2. Think about how markets of different sizes relate to one another, and how those relationships can impact your ability to get started.

6

What Your Product Enables

*"New products and services win in the marketplace if they help cus-
tomers get a Job done better (faster, more predictably, with higher
output) and/or more cheaply."* – Tony Ulwick, Strategyn Founder &
CEO

On its own, technology isn't worth very much.

Products and technology gain most of their value when they unlock new
potential: when they allow people to get better results, do things more quickly,
more conveniently, at lower costs, or with greater precision.

Every day, we're faced with thousands of Jobs—things we try to accomplish
in a given situation as per the Job to be Done theory—in our work, leisure, or
personal lives. We use different tools, products, services, or solutions to get
those Jobs done.

As an example:

My manager needs to show progress for our marketing team. He
asks me (the Job Performer) to create a presentation (the Job)[27].

I'm hoping to get promoted later this year (personal motivation). I look for ways to create a remarkable presentation, and get noticed (desired outcomes). There are multiple things that I need to do to prepare the presentation (the Job process).

I generally use many tools and products (solution) to create new decks. Throughout the project, I'm likely to encounter various issues (problems); each of the tools and products I use—Photoshop, Excel, PowerPoint, etc—will either help or hinder the Job that I'm trying to get done.
I expect certain outcomes from each of these products. My manager and the executive team will also have their expectations (desired outcomes). For me to consider using a new product given the pressure that I'm under (circumstances), there needs to be significant upside (differentiated value) considering that failing isn't an option (risk).

New benefits could potentially be: speeding up the creation process; helping make the presentation more engaging; creating a more professional-looking deck; or helping better communicate the key facts. I don't care equally about these benefits. Neither will my manager. Therefore, a product that sells me on being able to create a more professional-looking deck may not be very appealing if I, myself, am a professional designer (personal situation).

This can be a lot to unpack, but let's break it down...

A Breakdown

People want to get Jobs done. Jobs can be anything from listening to music, to filing taxes, to creating a presentation, to a million other things. They *hire* products—or other types of solutions like services or custom processes—to get those Jobs done. The Job is always independent from the solution.

The performance of those *solutions* is evaluated by how well they meet the needs. The evaluation criteria used are usually called needs or desired outcomes. A product typically addresses many desired outcomes.

Problems and obstacles hinder the progress that we're trying to make. These problems can be anything from minor annoyances—before, during, or after trying to get the Job done—to major blockers that completely prevent the completion of the Job.

People tend to overvalue their current solutions[28], whatever those are, and they tend to default to the status quo.

If a technology or innovation can help someone get an important Job done significantly better—often by a factor of 10x[29]—based on his or her own evaluation criteria, then they'll at least *consider* making a change.

Trying (or buying) products in B2B is sometimes limited by the perception of risk or the complexity of convincing a group of stakeholders (team members, for example) to make a change. This fact can never be understated.

If you know what Job customers might hire your product for, and how they might evaluate its use or value, then you can find the right market for it.

Where it Starts

At this stage, we're in a bit of a chicken and egg situation. If we don't know the exact people or persona that our innovation helps, then it's hard to know what kind of value they will agree to pay for, or in what context our innovation will be most valuable.

If you've made it this far with your innovation, typically you'll be in one of two situations:

1. **You'll know the value**: You have a good idea of the type of value that your innovation can deliver. This value might come from solving a pain point, removing blockers, delivering new outcomes, or improving performance. You might not know in which context this value will be most valuable, or who will benefit most, but based on your understanding of the value, you will be able to discover this optimal context and, ultimately, the right market for your innovation. This is the challenge that Flutura (Chapter #14), Psykler (Chapter #9), and Superpowered had to overcome; *or*

2. **You'll know the Job**: Alternatively, you might know the Job that your solution addresses, but you may not know what market(s) perform that Job, or what specific benefits influence prospects' purchase decisions. Based on the Job that you have identified, you can find the most promising market opportunities and the best benefits to put forth. This is the situation that Algolia (Chapter #7), TensorGraph (Chapter #11), and Veeva Systems (Chapter #5) found themselves in.

In essence, the objective of this section is to help you find the best possible combination of a market (who your innovation helps), Job to be Done (when it helps), and value (what specific value it delivers):

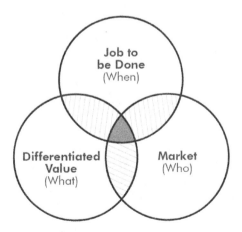

Figure 6.1 – A Job, differentiated value, and market segment combination

Since these three assumptions will be interlinked, they should be tested together with prospects in the market.

So, *do you know what Job your innovation helps with? Do you know what value your innovation delivers?*

No matter what your starting point is, your assumptions will need to be fleshed out.

Job Assumptions

Jobs aren't made up. And technology products rarely find a use without a customer need.

If you are to succeed with your innovation, someone somewhere must already be addressing—or at least trying to address—the Job that your product enables.

There might not be an existing product category for it, but any Job that matters will already be addressed in some capacity, whether it's through a manual process, a multi-tool solution, a custom-built tool, or a competing product.

As positioning expert April Dunford says in her book, *Obviously Awesome*: "*It's important to really understand what customers compare your solution with, because that's the yardstick they use to define "better.""*

Jobs can be functional (what customers want to get done), emotional (how customers want to feel or avoid feeling as a result of executing the functional Job), or social (how customers want to be perceived by others). However, it's the functional Job that tends to define the playing field of an innovation.

At this stage, you need to define the functional Job that your product enables. Jobs are best expressed as follows[30]:

verb + object of the verb (noun) + contextual clarifier

For example, buy a car, create a presentation, listen to music while commuting to work, or plan annual vacations.

It's important to understand that products are made better in context of the Job that they enable. Slack, for example, is a better group chat **when a team is collaborating on work**, while WhatsApp is a better tool **when communicating with family members**[31]. If we remove products from their optimal contexts of use, it's quite likely that their value will be significantly reduced.

The circumstances—or contextual clarifier—help to point out the context that makes your product a winning solution. For example:

Create a presentation **when running out of time**

There could be several solutions for this Job:

- hiring a team of designers to create the presentation;
- buying a templated presentation;
- using Photoshop, Excel, and PowerPoint; or
- *hiring* a new technology product.

For now, write down the core functional Job that your product enables, and start thinking about the competing solutions for that Job. The value of your innovation will be easier to understand once we compare it with other possible solutions for the Job.

Value Assumptions

How does your innovation make performing the Job better? Does it make it faster? Cheaper? Does it help remove blockers? How does this value compare to the other solutions available?

According to research by innovation consulting firm Strategyn[32], most Jobs, even simple ones, have 50–150 desired outcomes. This means that there might be as many as 150 different ways to deliver more value for the same Job.

Some of these outcomes will be trivial, while others will have the potential to deliver a significant ROI.

Delivering incredible amounts of value around a trivial outcome might never move the needle enough to get prospects to adopt a new product. This is why, early on when trying to establish a beachhead, your innovation needs to deliver a significant—10x—improvement around a key evaluation criterion.

Although 10x may not always be possible, or necessary, it's a good rule to remind yourself that prospects won't make significant changes to the way they work to adopt products that are simply different, or slightly better.

To find your core value assumption, list every way in which your innovation improves the execution of the Job.

These improvements might be:

- **Process-driven**: reducing time, costs, errors, risk, uncertainty, or complexity; *or*
- **Outcome-driven**: increasing revenue, profits, opportunities, demand, reach, targeting, satisfaction, or value.

Opportunities can be revealed by comparing the performance of the alternatives around key evaluation criteria.

Which of your value assumptions is most compelling? Which is most differentiated? Which aligns with an important evaluation criterion for prospects? Are there any overlaps?

The greater the value gap (the differentiated value), the greater the likelihood that prospects will consider your solution.

VALUE HYPOTHESES	PAIN	DIFFERENTIATION	IMPACT
Decrease the complexity of keeping presentations in sync	3	3	2
Decrease the time needed to create a new presentation	6	8	7
Decrease the time needed to update presentations	4	4	4
Lower the cost of creating new presentations	3	6	6
Minimize the risk of data entry errors	2	4	2

Figure 6.2 – Example of a comparison of value assumptions

Getting back to our previous example, if our innovation uses artificial intelligence (AI) to turn Excel spreadsheets into PowerPoint presentations, the benefits could be:

· decreasing the time needed to create a new presentation;
· minimizing the risk of data entry errors;
· decreasing the time needed to update presentations;
· reducing the complexity of keeping presentations in sync; and
· lowering the cost of creating new presentations.

Prospects won't care equally about all of these benefits. The value you lead with should be the most compelling, and the one that is the most differentiated when compared with the alternatives.

By running the numbers and comparing solutions, we could hypothesize that our solution will significantly decrease the time needed to create a new presentation. We can make this our value assumption.

Your value assumption won't be perfect. As innovation expert Tristan Kromer says[33]: *"We cannot have a validated value proposition without a validated customer segment."* Both your Job and value assumptions will need to be validated in the market.

Case Study :: Locking in on the Core Value of Superpowered

Superpowered was founded by Patrick Vlaskovits and Gábor Szántó.

Although the company was started in 2013, the seed of Superpowered's value was planted much earlier on.

In the mid-90s, Gábor, a Hungarian DJ and engineer would regularly over-clock his Celeron computer to write EDM music with FruityLoops[34]. These early experiments introduced him to the importance of CPU meters and performance in music creation. They would also become instrumental to Superpowered's success.

When the first major mobile platforms were coming out, it was clear to Gábor that DJ tools were going to move to mobile.

Having thought that he could create his own simply by finding an audio engine and wrapping it into a user interface, Gábor was shocked to realize that none of the existing engines performed well on low-powered devices like the iPhone.

Tapping into his unique experiences, Gábor created his own audio engine which, in 2008, allowed him to launch a DJ app that could rival laptop performances.

The app, DJ Player, became a major hit. Yet, in spite of the accolades, Gábor felt that the engine could do even more.

Wanting to bring his creation to market, Gábor convinced entrepreneur and bestselling author Patrick Vlaskovits to join up.

Although Gábor's experiences had shown that a lower latency audio engine requiring less power would be valuable, in 2013 they were several years ahead of the market.

To bridge the gap, Patrick set to work. Through early sales and customer interviews, he was able to learn that their software development kit (SDK) would be more valuable to Android developers.

On Android, developers had to deal with fragmentation, development was a mess, and when projects were multi-platform, Superpowered's SDK significantly gained in value.

The more they refined their targeting and honed in on the prospects that they could help (their MVS), the more the market caught on.

Building off their core paid off. In 2020, Splice, the makers of a major music production platform, acquired Superpowered. The same core that was discovered through experimentation in the 90s and refined over the years led to their acquisition more than 20 years later.

Looking back, Patrick says[35]: *"There's only a few characteristics of audio that people care about. There's the subjective audio experience. But it's well understood that audio has to be interactive and low latency. And then it's bit depth and things like that. [...] People are always going to look at the same parameters and compare it to their solutions."*

Just as Patrick and Gábor were able to do, you'll need to narrow down the list of attributes that prospects value. These attributes will ultimately help you find the best opportunity for your product.

Putting it All Together

Superpowered is a good example of a startup that started with a strong innovation and a good sense of the value that their technology could deliver.

Through interviews and sales conversations, the founders were able to identify the Job and the specific context in which their product's value would be most compelling (multi-platform development).

These insights helped the founders home in on market segments that could benefit from their product in the short term.

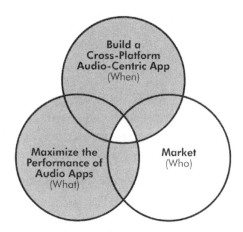

Figure 6.3 – Superpowered's Job and value assumptions

To start finding markets for your innovation, clarify the Job that your solution enables and the value that you intend to deliver. This pairing will help structure your search for a market in the next chapter.

Taking Action (2 hours)

1. Define the Job that your product enables. Identify the circumstances that make your product gain in value.
2. Understand the other solutions that prospects might hire for the same Job.
3. Clarify the value of your innovation. Evaluate how differentiated that value might be from the prospect's perspective.

7

Value/Market Assumptions

"The age old question of do you want to take a small piece of a big market or a big piece of a small market is a strategic trap. You want a piece of a market that is artificially small now and will become big later with the right product.[36]*"* – Aaron Levie, Box CEO & Co-Founder

In many ways, new innovations are exciting for the same reason why they're difficult: possibilities.

The more *generalized* an innovation is, the more possibilities there are. Yet many entrepreneurs and innovators, when faced with the exciting prospect of new inventions, tend to limit their own exploration (due to lack of time, awareness, or interest). But limiting market exploration sometimes also means limiting potential.

Different applications of new technologies will yield different outcomes. As an example, in my book *Solving Product*, I covered the story of Poppulo, an email marketing platform (red ocean) that pivoted into internal communications (blue ocean), a nascent market with much less competition. The same base technology in a different market created a different upside.

If a market is underserved, or if a segment experiences the problem more acutely, then prospects may be willing to engage with startups much earlier on, or to spend more money for a solution that's just *good enough*.

Exploring a broader set of markets is, at the very least, a good risk management strategy. Not only will it help you to chart your market expansion strategy, it reduces the risk of being blindsided by better opportunities later on.

But to do any of that, first you need to start generating value/market assumptions.

Finding Markets

Finding the right MVS is a lot like sculpting.

For both activities, you start with a much broader piece than the end product will be. Through iterations and refinements—which exclude more and more of the market—the important details come into the light. And eventually, things click; the level of detail is just right and you're ready to start selling.

You can't guess your way to the exact right MVS. The markets that you'll be brainstorming in this chapter will be starting points, not end destinations. They'll be useful guides to tell you *where* to start digging.

To make sure that your market assumptions can be compared, you need to make sure that they're of the same level (industries vs industries, verticals vs verticals, etc).

If you were to compare, for example, the Oil & Gas industry to fly fishing experts in Vermont, then your results would, at best, be very misleading.

To make sure that you are covering your bases, and that you're exploring as broadly as possible, consider going through one, or several, of the following exercises.

As you go through the exercises, try to think of specific people and businesses in the markets. This will help keep you focused on how the Job and value might be experienced.

1. **Analyze related needs**: If we start with an example of machines over-heating, we can find markets by going upstream in the value chain. *What companies are selling these machines? In which other markets and industries are these companies selling?* Looking upstream can reveal markets by proxy. Thinking about complementary parts can also yield interesting markets. Ask yourself: *What other parts are needed to make these machines work? In what other markets are the makers of these products selling?* Looking at related needs or problems can help you tap into the market research of other organizations.

2. **Ask around**: Our own life experiences can help us identify certain markets, but they can also blind us to other opportunities. The easiest way to go beyond our own knowledge is to ask around. Describe the Job and the value of your technology in layman's terms to relationships, connections, and people in your team. *What markets do they come up with?* Take note of their suggestions. By tapping into other people's knowledge, you can significantly widen the scope of the opportunities that you consider. It's actually been shown through research that founding teams with more diverse life experiences will tend to identify more varied (and distant) market opportunities[37]. You can get similar value by asking around.

3. **Analyze social media**: In the previous chapter we identified some of the keywords that prospects might be using to search for our solution (e.g. creating presentations from Excel). Search engines and social media platforms (e.g. Twitter, Reddit, Quora, etc) can help us discover prospects that are already talking about these topics, or even better, who are in the market looking for a solution. *Can you find their profiles? In*

what markets would they fall? How would you categorize them?

4. **Leverage market and industry lists**: To further extend your search, consider going through industry and market lists. Government or economic development organizations like the Government Census Data, the World Bank, or the IMF often have hierarchical lists that can be browsed or searched. The US government, the UK government, and the European Union also have lists that are available for free[38]. Alternatively, sites like LinkedIn are structured around business markets, while social network platforms like Quora, Reddit, or Pinterest are structured around hobbies and interests. *Can these sites help you come up with a few more assumptions?*

Come up with 30–40 market assumptions. Don't try to push your search too far. You'll probably start seeing diminishing returns on your efforts once you've come up with 20–30 assumptions.

We'll start prioritizing the list in the next chapter.

Case Study :: How Psykler Brainstormed Market Opportunities

During the writing of *Lean B2B*, I was approached by the founder of Psykler, a relationship profiling tool used during complex sales processes.

At the time, the founder, Wayne McIntyre, had already signed customers in pharma, aviation, and contract research. Although the company had revenue, product usage was low, and there was no indication that Psykler had PMF with any of its customers.

I agreed to help Wayne and his team carve their best path forward. Since Psykler only had one client in each market, and a lot of the early sales had come from Wayne's prior consulting engagements, it made sense to take a step back.

By sitting down with the founder, and analyzing the data gathered through discussions, interviews, and the past year of operation, we identified the context in which we felt that sales staff would most benefit from a relationship profiling tool like Psykler.

We looked for industries where salespeople sold face-to-face, where deals were above $100,000, and where more than 50 relationships had to be developed. Those were all informed *theories* about Psykler's ideal end users.

These criteria helped us identify 42 markets in which we felt Psykler might be valuable.

To find the most promising, we listed the 12 criteria we felt were most important. The criteria ranged from company size to current budget for sales data tools. They also included more specific criteria such as the structure of the sales team, whether or not they collaborated on deals, and the importance they gave to sales effectiveness.

To limit guesswork, we looked at specific companies in each market and gathered a lot of data through secondary research. Lastly, we prioritized the criteria amongst themselves, and weighted our rankings.

After a thorough analysis, the industries that topped our list were pharma, enterprise software, consulting, and integrators. Only one of Psykler's original customers was in these markets. This meant that we would most likely end up taking a step back.

To further narrow down our list, we followed our analysis with a short series of interviews in each market, as you'll see in Chapter #9. These interviews helped us refine our targeting and lock in on our most promising market opportunities. Soon, you'll be able to do the same.

Taking Action (2 hours)

1. Use your Job and value assumptions to come up with a list of 30–40 markets.
2. Go through the various brainstorming exercises in this chapter to maximize the number and range of opportunities that your team considers.

8

Prioritizing Market Assumptions

"You're not obligated to serve every possible customer. The products and services you develop should match your company's overall financial and commercial goals." – Madhavan Ramanujam and Georg Tacke, Authors of Monetizing Innovation

You've been able to identify a few dozen markets. Many look promising. *How do you know which to focus on?*

I'm sorry to say, but at this point, there is **no** perfect formula. There's only the formula that's right for now.

The factors that you use to prioritize market assumptions should change based on your timeline, your need for capital, your market knowledge, your goals, and the specifics of your business strategy.

For example, if you're in a cash crunch, you'll probably want to go after markets with fewer decision-makers and prospects that can easily be reached and sold to. This, in turn, would help improve your ability to generate revenue quickly, and your odds of survival.

Alternatively, if like Unitychain (Chapter #12) your technology gains in value when more people use it, you may decide to prioritize acquiring large numbers of users over generating revenue.

There are many critical and situational factors that are worth considering in your prioritization. In this chapter, we'll cover both categories, to help you find the best way to prioritize your market assumptions.

Critical Prioritization Factors

Critical factors are factors that are important no matter what kind of business you're building.

For example, your business will never grow quickly if you can't reach the buyers. Alternatively, if a market is overserved and the needs are well satisfied by competing solutions, then you'll have a hard time carving out a niche in the market. Ease of reach and Competition are both critically important factors.

If you decide to ignore critical factors, make sure you're doing it in full awareness of the risks that you are introducing in your model.

In *Crossing the Chasm*, Geoffrey Moore recommends evaluating markets using six key criteria. These criteria include:

1) Compelling Reason to Buy

Everything starts with value. If your product doesn't solve the right pains, or deliver the right gains, you'll have a hard time getting any sort of traction in the market.

If your product's value isn't meaningful at all, prospects simply won't buy. However, if it has *some*—not significant—value, you might not be able to tell quickly.

The difference between selling a hard benefit (with tangible returns on investment that can be demonstrated) and selling a soft benefit (one that's harder to quantify, and can be deemed a nice-to-have) is key.

Going after markets that experience the pain more acutely and/or will get an outsized amount of value significantly improves your odds of success.

When you have a compelling value proposition, prospects are more responsive, more likely to follow up, more willing to prioritize your solution, more likely to do the selling for you—and if your product does deliver value, they'll be more likely to refer it to others.

Will your solution provide real value? Will it provide quantifiable benefits? Will you be able to demonstrate that value? Can prospects decide to do nothing?

2) Budget

If you want to build a business, you need to be able to get paid for the value that you create. Without a revenue model, a product is just a hobby.

If customers don't have money, if they don't pay for products, or if they're in cost-saving mode, you'll have a hard time reaching your financial goals.

Markets that are expanding, with many businesses that are well capitalized and growing, can be more forgiving and willing to spend more on innovative products. With more money, you can hire more engineers, spend more on customer acquisition, or take home more profits. Generating more revenue than your competitors can be a true advantage on the market.

Do prospects gladly pay for tools and solutions? Do they have budgets? Is their revenue growing, or declining? Will there be enough prospects with money to sustain your business?

Although the markets that you consider don't *all* need to be flush with cash, there should be enough revenue for you to be able to create a sustainable business.

3) Ease of Reach

You don't sell to Fortune 500 companies in the same way you sell to startups—and you don't sell to the CEOs of SMBs the way you sell to C-Level executives.

Your market, the price of your solution, and the budget that you're targeting will determine the people you need to sell to. If your buyer is hard to reach, or if the organization has well-established purchasing processes, you'll generally need to deal with longer sales cycles.

Early on, you need to decide whether you want to sell big, or sell fast. As a rule, it's difficult to do both at the same time. *How are the organizations in the market structured? Do they have procurement departments? In what team or department would your buyer be? Would you be able to reach them directly? What would need to happen for you to be able to do that consistently?*

There needs to be a path for your team to reach the right decision-makers in a timely fashion, and at a cost that makes sense for your business model. If buyers aren't reachable, or if the business model can't make sense downstream, you'll have a hard time capturing a large share of the market within a reasonable time frame.

4) Whole Product

There are markets that you could win next year by changing large parts of your product, there are markets that you could win in three months by making *some* adjustments, and then there are markets that you could win today with the product that you currently have.

To be able to gain a foothold in the market, you need the *Whole Product*—the minimum set of requirements (features, certifications, partnerships, etc.) required to convince businesses to work with you—or you should at least be very close to having everything they need.

To go fast, you should go after markets that you can satisfy today with your product and the help of partners and integrations. Although there may be more promising markets that require a different feature set, it makes sense to prioritize markets in which you can compete in the near term.

Never underestimate the effort required to get your product market-ready. It's important to account for both product and distribution challenges that need to be overcome to enter the market.

Will there be design or user interface challenges? Are there regulation requirements that will need to be addressed? Are there technological challenges that will be amplified if you enter this market? What gaps will need to be filled? Are there ways to work with partners to fill those gaps?

The importance you put on having the Whole Product is ultimately a time to market decision.

5) Competition

Early on, you won't be competing on equal footing. Other vendors will have had more time to build awareness, develop relationships with customers, learn, and build the assets they need to win.

Entering a market that is well established and already has entrenched competition requires strong differentiation, or an advantage unique enough to convince prospects to choose your solution over the incumbents'.

Although this isn't impossible to do, it can be much faster (and easier) to go after markets that are less competitive, or where competitors are showing signs of stagnation, or moving slowly.

Ultimately, whether you choose to go after a market that has few or many competitors, you need to make sure that you are entering a market that you can win.

As management expert Constantinos C. Markides says[39]: *"There is no point rushing into a new market unless you have a way to beat the existing players at their own game."*

So, *who are the competitors? Would they be* **direct** *competitors? Would you be able to compete against them? Could you actually win?*

6) Market Leadership

Companies build a lot of assets and resources in the process of developing markets (expertise, thought leadership, brand, connections, pipelines, visibility, collaterals, functionalities, etc). When their market expansion strategies are well thought out, these assets compound and help accelerate the growth.

However, when companies have built brand, leadership, and expertise in markets that are either too unique, or that are negatively perceived, they can end up limiting their ability to expand into new markets.

An interesting example of this challenge is content subscription service company OnlyFans, which gained visibility and profitability by targeting the adult industry. As it tries to expand into more conventional markets, the question of whether or not their brand and notoriety will limit their ability to win more mainstream[40] audiences is open to debate.

The markets you choose to prioritize should help to open new market opportunities. At this stage, it's important to understand the type of customers that will be guided by your early customers' purchase decisions. Your brand, expertise, network, case studies, and product functionalities should help open new doors for you, not close them.

Situational Prioritization Factors

The previous factors are all critical. However, due to your current strategy, your funding situation, your personal interests, or your domain expertise, it may be that other, more situational, factors will point to markets that are better fits right now.

Consider using some of the factors in this section or adding your own. As an example, early on, the founding team of Flutura (Chapter #14) chose to prioritize opportunities based on the amount of value that their solution unlocked or the intensity of the pain—whether the solution was perceived as a 'Vitamin' or a 'Pain Killer', whether someone would get promoted by solving the problem, whether the organization had enough data to solve the problem, and whether simply living with the pain (e.g. status quo) was an option.

Your prioritization should reflect your current business strategy.

Market Size

The most common way to evaluate markets is by their size. This is the reason why the idea of *Total Addressable Market* introduced in Chapter #5 is so alluring.

Large markets can be interesting down the road, but early on, size can actually be detrimental to your growth. Large markets have generally already attracted well-capitalized competitors; they'll have more noise. To be able to establish your beachhead, you should go after markets that you can win quickly.

Now, perhaps even more important than the size of a market is its growth rate (current and expected). Selling into a mature market, which is either growing slowly or regressing, forces you to convince organizations that have already made their purchase decision to make a switch and adopt a new solution.

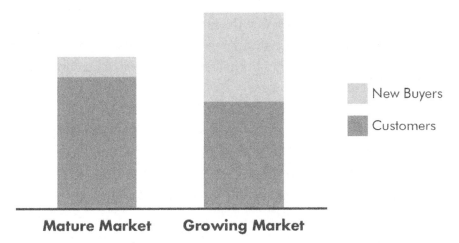

Mature Market   Growing Market

Figure 8.1 – Customer acquisition in growing and stagnant markets

If the market is growing quickly, there is likely to be a healthy stream of new organizations that have yet to make a commitment. It's usually easier for organizations to add new technology products, than to replace them.

Consider prioritizing markets based on the overall market size, and/or the market's expected growth rate.

Prior Market or Industry Experience

You might have an advantage or a disadvantage in some of the markets that you choose to prioritize.

When founding teams enter markets that they already understand, or in which they have prior experience, they tend to find their bearings faster and adapt more quickly. If their networks also connect them to prospects and influencers, they also have an advantage.

Although it may make sense to target markets that are promising but require more learning later, in the early stages the learning cost may be too significant to handle. It's been proven[41] that the further removed a founding team's experience is from the market that they are targeting, the longer it will take for them to build relationships, to understand the market dynamics, and to build the right product.

In general, it's better to target markets in which your know-how and expertise can be advantages. However, if you have the time, and you feel that the investment can ultimately pay off, it can be a good idea to include opportunities that push beyond your current experiences and expertise.

The decision to (de)prioritize markets in which you have experience is really a time to product/market fit decision.

Time to Product/Market Fit

To find PMF you need to be able to iterate a lot with a lot of customer feedback.

Beyond making sure that you have the Whole Product, the best way to speed up your time to product/market fit (TTPMF)—the time that it takes you to find PMF—is by prioritizing markets in which you can have a lot of face-time with prospects.

Targeting organizations that are smaller or less constrained in how they can work with technology vendors can help create better feedback loops.

This may allow you to visit customers at their worksites or have regular calls with them, or perhaps you could set up a customer development panel[42] with your best users. This, in turn, will help you to gain the knowledge you need rapidly, and feed your iteration cycles.

On the other hand, if the markets you choose prevent you from getting close to the customer—as might be the case in regulated industries—then this will limit the rate at which you are able to learn and iterate, and ultimately grow and fund your business. TTPMF is often an important consideration in the early days of startups.

Time to Cashflow

How long will it take you to reach the decision-makers? Can prospects buy their own solutions? Will purchases need to get escalated? Do customers already have a budget to solve this pain? How many people need to get involved in order for a sale to close? Does it need to go through procurement? How long does it take for you to receive payment once a deal closes?

For startups, cash is oxygen. If you're bootstrapping, or if your funding situation isn't secure, it may make sense to prioritize markets based on the time needed from initial prospect interaction to payment receipt. Businesses can implode or come to a standstill when they can't make payroll. If you need to factor in cashflow in the near term, consider prioritizing markets in which sales close quickly and payment terms can be advantageous (e.g. annual contracts).

As a rule, the fewer teams, people, or departments need to be involved in the purchasing process, the faster deals close—and the fewer checks and balances there are, the better the payment terms can be.

It can take a while to build cashflow. If you have raised capital and you're not in a cash crunch, time to cashflow might not be a priority at the moment.

Interest

Last, but not least, it's important to remember that businesses are social endeavors, built and operated by humans.

Most human beings find greater enjoyment and motivation when they're helping people and businesses that they care about.

It may take years for your company to win its core market—and if you or your partners aren't genuinely interested in the problems and reality of a market, not only will prospects feel it, you'll also have a hard time learning fast, and sustaining momentum when the going gets tough.

If you already have investors, advisors, partners, and employees, it makes sense to consider the alignment of their interests when deciding which markets to focus on. Investors, for example, may have decided to invest *because* of the market that you were going after. In that case, not only should they be involved in the decision-making process, they should also probably take part in the prioritization.

Don't disregard the human side of building a business. People's incentives and motivations need to align in order for a business to go fast.

Case Study :: Why Algolia Prioritized Recognizable Brands

Gaëtan Gachet joined Algolia, a site search startup based in Paris, in November 2013.

At the time, the company had a product, but they were barely making any revenue[43]. The technology, the founders' ambitions, and their desire to scale internationally had convinced Gaëtan to join the company.

After spending five years doing outbound sales in California, Gaëtan had recently returned to France, where he was looking for a new challenge. And what a challenge it would be…

Algolia's goal for 2014 was to reach $1M in annual recurring revenue (ARR).

To reach that goal, Gaëtan knew that they would need answers to the following questions: *Was Algolia an enterprise or a SMB product? Should they be targeting specific verticals, or should they offer a more generalized solution? Should they focus on certain use cases? What problem were they solving? Who were their customers? And had they found PMF, or not?*

Gaëtan says: *"When you put yourself in such a high growth mode, you completely change the way you operate. You make decisions much quicker. […] Fail fast, that's really what we did."*

Early on, it became clear that selling to large French companies would be just as difficult as selling to large American companies. The difference, however, was that American brands would be recognizable globally. By starting in the US, they could sign customers whose visibility would help them land even more customers globally.

Instead of focusing on a specific niche, they let the market choose them. This, in turn, allowed them to test different positionings, and use cases that pointed to the most promising opportunities.

2014 turned out to be the year of rejection. But through countless pitches, Gaëtan learned what customers valued and how to best sell their technology. By the end of the year, they had exceeded their objective and landed over 400 clients, including well-known brands like Product Hunt.

By landing these early customers, and leveraging their visibility, Algolia's international growth was accelerated. Today, Algolia has more than 8,000 customers, including some of the world's most recognizable companies like

Stripe, Sephora, Lacoste, and Slack[44].

Shortlisting Markets

Once you know which factors you want to use for your prioritization, then you need to prioritize these factors.

Is targeting a large market the most important thing to you? Is it critical that your early customers are recognizable brands as it was for Algolia?

Knowing which factors matter most to your team will help you to make better decisions. However, since at this stage we're really just dealing with assumptions, it's important to understand that stacking more assumptions doesn't create more objectivity. All it can do is give *the appearance* of certainty.

So resist the urge to calculate scores, or to create a prioritization algorithm. Simply add the list of markets that was brainstormed in the previous chapter to a spreadsheet and assign scores from one to ten for each factor (ten being the highest).

You can create your own spreadsheet, or you can download our template at findyourmarket.co/markets.

Review markets one at a time. Make a qualitative determination by weighing the pros and cons of each market, using all the information at your disposal.

MARKET	EXAMPLE	YOU CAN ACCESS IT	COMPELLING VALUE PROPOSITION	WHOLE PRODUCT IN PLACE	DIFFERENTIATED PRODUCT	OPENS NEW OPPORTUNITIES
Advertising agency	Sid Lee					
Aerospace	CAE					
Business aviation services	ExecAir					
Clean tech services	BioAmber					
Commercial insurance sales (small brokerage)	Aviva					
Commercial insurance sales	Marsh					
Construction	SNC Lavalin					
Consulting companies	McKenzie					
Consulting engineering services	CIMA					
Contract research	Charles River					
Corporate real estate	Colliers					
Defence	Lockheed					
Education technology providers	Nendle					
Enterprise software	RelateIQ					
Event planning	JPDL					
Financial software providers	Black line					
Food services	Aramark					
Health care software	Caristix					

Figure 8.2 – Example of a market prioritization sheet

Shortlist the three to five most promising markets and move on. Don't overcomplicate this process. We'll start exploring the markets to gather real facts about them in the next chapter.

◀◀

If, after the prioritization, the markets at the top of your list don't feel very compelling, consider getting back to the drawing board (Chapter #7) to come up with new market assumptions.

Taking Action (2 hours)

1. Familiarize yourself with the factors that have been outlined in this chapter. Select the most meaningful, based on the unique dynamics of your business. Consider adding your own.
2. For each market, assign a score per factor.
3. Qualitatively assess markets by comparing scores and the information at your disposal.
4. Select the three to five most promising markets and move forward.

9

Exploring Markets

"Don't ignore the unexpected, it's the richest source of innovation." – Peter Drucker, Management Consultant

You have identified several markets that look promising. *Now what? What signals would confirm market promise? What information would make you invalidate the market? How can you further refine your list?*

Look back at Chapter #6—to be interesting, a market needs to have:

1. **The existence of the Job to be Done**: Companies or people within the market must perform—or be attempting to perform—the core Job that your technology enables. Perhaps they are currently doing the Job manually or using a competing product, or they may be in the market looking for a solution just like yours. If the Job isn't on their radar, you'll simply be wasting your time.

2. **Unmet needs or unrealized potential**: Your product or technology needs to solve problems with their existing solution, or be able to generate superior outcomes for them. Without differentiated value—or the promise of some form of ROI—you will have a hard time getting the attention of stakeholders, *and...* should your solution get adopted, you'll

struggle to cement your relationship with them.

3. **Budget**: You can hit a dead end fast if the prospects never pay for tools or products. Try to understand if a need is budgeted (for example if prospects currently hire consultants or pay for solutions to this need), or if a new budget would have to be created. This will help you further understand internal priorities, and in turn, this will allow you to get a feel for the sales cycle, should you decide to enter this market later on.

4. **A catalyst for change**: Although you may never sell to the organizations that you'll be speaking with, there must be some sort of momentum driving the organization to make a change. *Perhaps the Job to be Done was prioritized in the New Year? Perhaps a new employee is driving change internally? Perhaps the current situation was made intolerable by outside pressures like competition or a change in market dynamics?* Whatever the reason, there needs to be some form of energy driving change inside the organization.

Things often look very different on the ground when you start interacting with prospects. Suddenly, you may realize that a certain market doesn't value the Job very much, or that there's very little pull for a technology product like yours.

At this stage, your goal is to gather as much information as possible. Doing so will help you identify promising segments, further refine your market list, and make decisions.

Who to Reach out to

To start learning, you need to speak to the right people. The bigger the companies are, however, the harder it will be to identify the right people to speak to.

As general rules of thumb, you'll want to reach out to:

- **CEOs or founders for companies with 100 employees or less**: At this size, companies rarely have more than three hierarchical levels. It's still possible for one central person (e.g. the CEO) to be aware of everything that goes on in the organization;
- **Functional leaders (e.g. Sales or Engineering leaders) for organizations with 100–250 employees**: As companies grow, they begin hiring more specialized functional leaders. Once that starts to happen, it's no longer realistic to expect the CEO or members of the founding team to still be keenly aware of everything the company is involved in;
- **[_____] in organizations with over 250 employees**: Because new layers of management get added, company structures don't line up from one company to the next, and reorgs often mix up staff responsibilities and hierarchies, so when there are over 250 employees, the right stakeholders generally need to be discovered.

It will often be easier—and faster—to get in touch with smaller organizations. If that's not possible for the markets that you are exploring, then you might need to use interviews to find the right roles inside organizations.

Alternatively, you may be able to find the right person by sending an email (or calling) your best guess for the right stakeholder inside the company. A script like the following can be really effective to start learning:

> Subject: quick question
>
> Hi [Maria],
>
> We have a product that we think can really help [Company].
>
> Would you guide me to the person responsible for [Job to be Done] and let me know the best way to get in touch with him or her?
>
> Let me know, thank you.

You can use LinkedIn, LinkedIn Sales Navigator, professional association directories, or any other watering holes to build your prospect lists. Once you know who you'd like to recruit, you can use tools like Hunter, ZoomInfo, Voila Norbert, or Clearbit Connect to quickly find their email addresses.

Recruiting Prospects for Interviews

Your goal is to interview five to seven prospects in each market. This number of prospects will help you balance *learning fast* and *learning the right things.*

Although you can use LinkedIn, Twitter, Quora, or the telephone for recruitment, cold emails are generally fast and effective. Because of this, they're always my *go-to.*

With qualified prospects, good credibility, and the right email script, you can expect a 10–20% contact-to-interview success rate. Based on the number of prospects you're trying to interview, this usually means finding 50 contacts per market, all in different companies.

For reach outs, you can use a template like the following, or you can create your own:

Subject Line: [International growth]

Hi [Max],

[I enjoyed your two-part series on employee retention. I had also tried to find a job in Hong Kong when I was living there. I know it's not easy.]

I'm contacting you because I have a software company trying to improve [how businesses expand internationally].

I'm not looking to sell anything, but since you have so much expertise with [international growth], I'd love to get your input to make sure we don't build the wrong thing.

Can I schedule a quick call with you next week? [Monday or Tuesday]?

Let me know, thank you.

Étienne

Make sure that you personalize the message, and that you use a custom lead-in as your intro. I like to establish the topic of discussion directly in the subject line—such as *International growth* in the above example.

You can download an editable copy at findyourmarket.co/template. For more instructions on recruiting interview participants via cold email, you can refer to our guide at findyourmarket.co/coldemails.

Conducting Interviews

Your goal with these interviews is to learn. Not to sell. Not to talk about your product.

Given how little time you'll have with each prospect (usually 20 mins), it's important to focus your enquiry on the key questions that will help you:

1. confirm the existence of the Job in the organization;
2. understand the circumstances and the Job Process; and
3. discover the current solutions and the unmet needs.

As you can see, none of these are specifically about your product or your innovation.

To avoid making wrong decisions, it's important to understand an organization's reality *before* assuming that there may be a fit for a solution like yours.

You can extract insights into budgets and pain points by listening to the interviewees' stories. But to get stories, you'll first need to make prospects talk.

Focus on asking open-ended questions (questions starting with *What*, *Why*, or *How*) and digging into the information prospects are giving you. If you're not sure how to conduct interviews, download our guide at findyourmarket.co/interviews.

You can get started with the following questions:

- *How would you describe your role as [Role]?*
- *What does success look like for you?*
- *Can you tell me how you deal with [Job to be Done]?*
- *Could you walk me through the last time you did [Job to be Done]? Who else got involved? What tasks were involved?*
- *What workarounds exist in your process?*
- *What problems are you trying to prevent or resolve?*
- *Talk me through how you currently work around [Specific Problem]?*
- *What makes [Job to be Done] better? What makes it worse?*
- *What products and services do you currently use to [Job to be Done]?*
- *How do you know you're doing the Job right?*
- *If for some reason you couldn't use [Current Solution] to help you [Job to be Done], what else would you use?*
- *When was the last time you tried to find a solution to [Job to be Done]?*
- *What happened to prompt that thought?*
- *What was wrong with what you were using?*
- *What alternatives did you consider?*
- *What gaps did you perceive in those solutions?*

- *What were the key things that stood out? Why did they stand out?*
- *What does success look like when using this type of solution?*

If you're not sure you're speaking to the right stakeholder—or you think that there might be a better person to speak with—consider asking:

Within the organization, who's responsible for [Job to be Done]?

If the answer is "no one", then the Job either doesn't exist, or it's not a priority.

Now, if they say "someone else", take note of their answer, and consider refocusing your reach outs around that specific profile.

Complete all interviews before making any decisions.

Analyzing the Results

It's easy to get excited when you are learning from the market. Your interviews might have revealed several opportunities that closely align to the value of your product, and your head may be spinning.

Try to put some time between finishing the interviews and starting your analysis. To avoid jumping to conclusions too quickly, consider bringing in teammates or advisors that weren't involved in the interview process. Listen to the interviews anew.

As a first step, take note of the interviewees whose organization had the *exact* Job or who did a Job that was very similar. *Did the Job feel critical? How were they addressing it? How were they evaluating the success of their solution(s)? How do they know it's working?*

It's generally a good sign when the discussion sustained their interest, there were a lot of questions asked, and the same challenges were often being mentioned.

During the interview, *did they mention gaps or problems with their current solutions? How did their needs line up with your product's unique value? If they were to implement your solution, would they **actually** gain a lot of value? Would this be around an objective that they care about?*

You'll probably be wasting your time if the unique value of your solution won't deliver big gains or solve big pains associated with criteria that the interviewees care about.

Take note of the interviewees whose organizations had the *exact* Job, and that would *truly* benefit from your product's unique value:

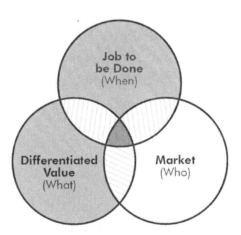

Figure 9.1 – Job and value assumptions

*What market or market grouping seem to be **causing** their need? Was this the top-level market that you had identified? Are there attributes or behaviors that seem to amplify their needs?*

Don't worry too much about the number of interviewees per grouping. These groupings are more signals than anything else.

If, like Psykler below, a particular segment of the market seems to be experiencing the need more acutely than others, then consider doing another round of interviews in that segment, so that you can refine your understanding.

If not, keep moving. We'll validate any market groupings that we identify in the coming chapters.

Case Study :: How Psykler Locked in on its MVS

At Psykler, after having narrowed the list of markets to just a few (Chapter #7), we began contacting prospects, cold calling organizations, trying to speak to as many salespeople as we could.

Within a week, we realized that sales staff in pharma, enterprise software, and integration rarely collaborated on deals. Since we believed that Psykler's profiling functionalities gained in value through collaboration, we decided to deprioritize these markets.

Although this could have forced us to take a step back, some of our interviews in consulting were showing promise.

Having recruited fairly broadly, we realized that some of our interviewees—those selling consulting services to slow-moving industries like healthcare, telcos, education, and defense—were facing major challenges.

In these markets, there were few prospects, deals involved many stakeholders, and opportunities to close deals were few and far between. Because they had to sell to large organizations with many stakeholders involved, sales were often complex, and this often triggered the need to collaborate on deals.

To sync up on strategy, they had account development meetings, and this was where we felt Psykler's relationship profiling tool would shine. Psykler would help them gain a better understanding of the stakeholders they were trying to sell to, and give them guidance on the best way to approach them.

We organized more interviews within these customer groups, so we could better understand their reality. Very quickly, we learned that upsell and long-term relationships were especially key in the services sector. In services, being more in tune with the needs and realities of your customers can mean stealing large deals from competitors.

The more we learned, the more we realized that companies that sold strategic IT services like business intelligence or security were forced to sell high to CIOs, CTOs, or VPs of Technology. Because there were so few opportunities to get in a room with these stakeholders, there was a much greater incentive to get the discussions to go well.

After a month of interviews, it was clear that Psykler, in its current form, was best suited to meet the needs of consulting firms selling in the security industry. These companies held account development meetings, they collaborated on relationship-building strategies, they had money, they were in pain, and they could reap tangible benefits from increasing their certainty. We decided to make this grouping our MVS.

As we refined our pitch and our understanding of the segment, the product began to click with prospects. From there, it was about refining our product and marketing to meet the needs of the customers.

▶▶

If you're selling to consumers (B2C), or your product is very
transactional, targeting small businesses, feel free to skip over
the next chapter, picking back up at Chapter #11, Analyzing Your
Findings.

Taking Action (1 to 4 weeks)

1. For each market prioritized, recruit five to seven prospects using cold
   emails.
2. Conduct interviews to confirm the existence of the Job in the organization, to understand the circumstances, to map the Job process, and to
   discover the gaps and desired outcomes.
3. Analyze the results.

10

Finding the Buyers

"There are three key reasons to cut out an audience: they don't pay for things gladly, they're dead set against tools or ways of working (no matter how better they are), or you don't like them." – Amy Hoy, Serial Entrepreneur

As you were interviewing prospects, you may have felt a certain pull from different influences within organizations. Maybe those were:

- **Job performers**: There may be several teams or people in the organization that have to perform the Job to be Done, or the tasks of the Job may be split across different users or business units. If you weren't speaking with the actual Job performers, you'll have a hard time locking in on the full set of requirements.
- **Decision-Makers**: The interviewees may have also referred to other decision-making influences during your conversations. These could be the stakeholders who chose the current solution, the people who initiated the project, the budget owners, or some other type of decision-maker wielding influence over the project (managers, technical buyers, or economic buyers). Failing to understand their needs and perspectives may ultimately block your progress.

- **Gatekeepers (also known as saboteurs)**: Conversely, there may be other decision-makers with competing or conflicting agendas. For example, a manager wishing to keep costs low, a procurement team wanting to freeze spending, or another manager wishing to see his or her competing project claim the funding. Without a feel for the negative influences in the organization, you run the risk of targeting markets that are much more difficult to sell into than you would have liked.

Whether or not you've sensed these influences during your early discussions, you should dig into your most promising markets before committing fully.

To get a full picture of the internal dynamics, you need to switch up your questioning to try to understand two key, sometimes *distinct*, influences:

1. the problem owner; *and*
2. the budget owner.

Depending on how companies in the market are structured, either one of these may be the ultimate decision-maker for your solution.

Although there may ultimately be one, two, six, or more people[45] playing the role of these influences, it's important to be aware of who plays which role. Each of these stakeholders will have a different profile, and a different perspective on the problem, the goals, and the requirements.

The Problem Owner

The *problem owner* is the person who experiences the pain, or the person who is ultimately responsible for solving the problem, or for managing the Job.

In most organizations, priorities are set at the top. Then, goals are split up into teams and departments and tasks and responsibilities are delegated down the totem pole. For example, if customer retention was set as a priority in the

New Year, the customer success, product, and customer service teams may all have been assigned different facets of this same goal.

The strategies they use to address those goals may be defined at team or department level, and managers are then made accountable for solving problems and delivering outcomes around those goals. Depending on the objectives or the problem space, the actual problem owner may be completely different.

Ultimately, you want to speak to the right people. The problem owner is the person that might get fired or promoted based on whether or not the objective is met. This person may, however, not be the problem's budget owner.

It's important to make sure that the problem is a problem that the company as a whole wants to see solved, not just a *pet problem* that matters to just one person.

The Budget Owner

In organizations, budgets don't always follow responsibilities. For example, sales and marketing departments often have some of the largest budgets in product organizations[46], but this doesn't mean that building the product is any less important. Some goals simply require more budget.

This means that different departments—sometimes even managers within teams—will have different budgets and purchasing authorities. If the budget owner isn't the problem owner, he or she may have a different take on what the spending priorities should be. Ultimately, they may be able to kill purchase requests that are pulling on their budgets.

By understanding who the budget owner is and what the company's priorities are, you can uncover blockers. Obviously, companies generally prefer to invest in opportunities that are fully aligned with their priorities.

This is why it's so important to understand who the budget owner is, and whether or not their priorities are aligned with the value that your product delivers. If your company wants to make money, understanding the budget owner is critical.

Conducting Interviews

You can view this new series of interviews as an opportunity both to deepen your understanding of the inner mechanics of organizations, and to get more data.

If you have already conducted interviews as detailed in the previous chapter, then sort out the most promising markets thus far. For each of these markets, recruit another five to seven prospects.

The aims of this new series of interviews are, once again, to understand whether or not the Job matters, to uncover the needs and problems, and to learn about the budget and problem owners.

Use some of the questions from the previous interviews...

- *When was the last time you did [Job to be Done]?*
- *What were you trying to accomplish? What tasks were involved?*
- *What problems were you trying to prevent or resolve?*
- *When do you typically need to do [Job to be Done]?*
- *What makes [Job to be Done] better? What makes it worse?*

...and add some of the following questions, so you can learn more about internal processes and the stakeholders involved:

- *Who typically gets involved? At what points of [Job to be Done]?*
- *How many people are affected by the [Job to be Done / Problem]?*
- *What have you done so far to try and solve [Job to be Done / Problem]?*

- *Who would you say is most affected by [Job to be Done]?*
- *Who ultimately is responsible for [Job to be Done]?*
- *Whom else in your company should we be speaking with regarding [Job to be Done]?*
- *If you identify the need for a new product in your department, how does your team typically go about purchasing that solution?*
- *Who are the four or six people who will make the decision?*
- *How do you typically purchase new solutions?*
- *Is there a reason why your team hasn't [hired an external consultant / purchased a solution] to address [Job to be Done]?*
- *How does your team choose which products or solutions it uses for [Job to be Done]?*

Select the most appropriate questions to ask. Try to identify both the problem and the budget owners.

At the end of every interview, you should be able to tell whether or not the specific organization performs the Job, what gaps and problems they perceive (if any), who cares most about addressing these problems, and who ultimately gets to decide or veto the solutions that get used to perform the Job.

Analyzing the Data

For each organization interviewed, fill out a buying influencer map, listing out the roles of every stakeholder involved:

COMPANY	INITIATOR		
WorkTag	Moritz Seidel, Director of Engineering		

PROBLEM OWNER	JOB PERFORMERS (USERS)	INFLUENCERS	DECISION-MAKERS
○ Moritz Seidel, Director of Engineering	○ Moritz Seidel, Director of Engineering ○ Paula Davis, Data Engineer ○ Mike Collins, Data Engineer ○ Lauren Ortiz, Sr. Data Engineer ○ Dawei Zhu, Architect	○ Julie Wójcik, VP of Engineering ○ Kim Breton, CTO ○ Mitchell Smith, Legal ○ Dawei Zhu, Architect	○ Karl Dalhouse, Director of Infrastructure ○ Julie Wójcik, VP of Engineering ○ Moritz Seidel, Director of Engineering

BUDGET OWNER	GATEKEEPERS	
Julie Wójcik, VP of Engineering	Ian McIntyre, VP of Strategy	

Figure 10.1 – Example of a buying influencer map

You can create your own template or you can download ours at findyourmarket.co/buyermap to get started fast.

Comparing maps per market, take note of variations in roles, structures, and influences: *How different are they across organizations? How many stakeholders typically get involved in decision-making? How distinct are the users, the problem owners, and the budget owners? Can problem owners generally make their own purchases? How difficult would it be to reach the decision-makers?*

The more stakeholders have to get involved, the greater the chances that their needs and agendas will conflict. Ideally, the user, the problem owner, and the budget owner are one and the same.

Although it's always possible to satisfy the needs of a group of stakeholders by addressing their individual needs, it can be better to avoid it.

Identify the markets with the simplest and the most complex breakdowns. Highlight stakeholders that will be difficult to reach and sell to. We'll put all of our data points together in the next chapter to start making decisions.

Case Study :: How Alex Berman Finds the Buyer in Large Organizations

Alex Berman is a go-to-market expert and the co-founder of Experiment 27, a company that helps businesses book meetings with billion-dollar brands.

Over the years, he has used his expertise in cold email marketing to land large clients, sell technology products, and purchase businesses.

To explore markets, Alex will generally send 100 cold emails per customer segment. Based on whether or not the prospects open the emails—and looking for open rates of 60–85%—he's able to get a feel for how challenging the prospects will be to reach.

Based on the email responses, he can also figure out which prospects have already bought (e.g. "Thanks, but we already have a vendor for this."), and which aren't interested.

The emails help him understand if he's on the mark, how engaged the prospects are, and whether or not they are committed with another vendor.

To find the right buyer, he usually starts top-down at the CEO level, sending his best messaging. If the CEO turns him down, he waits a few weeks, and then contacts the person at the next level down, usually a C-level executive. If this doesn't work, he waits another two weeks, and tries the next level down.

Alex says: *"I'm always surprised when [the emails] turn into meetings—not with the CEO, but with somebody multiple levels down."*

Alex will keep sending emails and working his way down until he reaches the exact team he's trying to sell to. Following this approach across multiple organizations helps him understand the internal structures on the market, and ultimately helps inform his go-to-market strategy.

In many ways, Alex has perfected the art of doing customer development via email.

Taking Action (1 to 2 weeks)

1. Familiarize yourself with the roles and responsibilities identified in prospect organizations.
2. Recruit five to seven prospects for each of the markets still in contention.
3. Conduct interviews to better understand the buying and decision-making processes inside organizations.
4. Create buying influencer maps to analyze the results of your research.

11

Analyzing Your Findings

"First-to-market matters, but so do many other things. Focus instead on being first to do something important 10x better.[47]" – Jason M. Lemkin

Here we are. In the span of just a few weeks, we have gone from having theories about how things *might be* in several markets, to having concrete primary data to help us make our decisions.

It's very likely that some of the markets that you have explored didn't look or feel the way you thought they would. Conversely, it's also possible that some of the markets you were exploring now feel much more promising than they once did. Things often look very different on the ground.

At this point, we now have:

1. a high-level assessment of each market's dynamics (Chapter #8);
2. detailed information about the needs and challenges of a small group of prospects in each market (Chapter #9); *and*
3. insights about budgets, purchasing authorities, and priorities (if you also did the research from Chapter #10).

It's now time to put everything together to further hone in on our MVS.

Revisit the spreadsheet that was created in Chapter #8, adding data points for each market. If you downloaded our template, you can simply switch to the next tab over.

At this point, don't give too much importance to the numbers of people that provided specific answers. Although you are trying to avoid edge cases, what you're really looking for are signals. Even small segments can be interesting. They can help you learn how to refine your targeting, and get to your MVS. We'll see how in the coming pages.

Finding the Sweet Spot(s)

How many markets are you still considering? Are there sub-segments within those markets that may be worth exploring?

You should keep segmenting the markets until you've locked in on:

1. *several* prospects who are trying to get the same value in a similar way;
2. in the same broader market that you could expand out of; and
3. with channels and the possibility of word of mouth between customers.

Your MVS should feel actionable; the value you need to deliver, the features you need to build, and the benefits sought should be clear to you.

If you found a few prospects that exhibited different behaviors, but seemed to see great value in your product, try to understand why. You may want to recruit more prospects like these for interviews, rather than discard their needs.

As we saw in the Psykler case study (Chapter #9), you could discover an attribute or a behavior that makes them see greater value in your technology.

For example, at Psykler we noticed that sales staff selling into certain industries exhibited different behaviors. Their teams had added an extra step to their sales process, which *we hypothesized* could be a great moment for them to use our relationship profiling tool.

Based on our discussions, it appeared that only certain types of businesses organized these meetings. Our new grouping was based on a hypothesis, which ultimately, after many conversations with prospects, was proven true.

It's a good idea to keep new segments separate from markets that you've already explored. You can treat them as new markets in your spreadsheet.

◀◀

If you feel like there are sub-segments of a market that may be worth exploring, jump back to Chapter #9 to interview more prospects in that specific segment.

Analyzing Your Markets

For a market to make sense, you need to have a path to entry, and a path to victory.

This means that your product's value must be compelling enough to get customers to adopt a new—and likely unproven—solution.

To get prospects to buy, the differentiated value must significantly outweigh the risks of buying from an unproven vendor and the full cost of switching (money, effort, resources, training, etc).

As a rule, this means delivering significant value—as much as 10x more value[48]—along a key evaluation criterion for the customer, while also meeting base expectations on other valued dimensions.

For example, if I am trying to sell you on a new email marketing platform—which is close to being a commodity these days—and I know that the way you evaluate the value of your platform is based on the revenue that you generate via email, then my product would need to help you generate significantly more revenue for it even to be considered.

You or members of your team would probably also want to do a careful comparison of platforms, evaluating them on the basis of other important dimensions, such as email deliverability rates, cost, customer service, and usability. By analyzing the added value, you can get a sense of whether or not customers would be willing to make a change.

There are always multiple forces at play, both pulling customers towards new products and preventing them from discarding their existing solutions. Your goal is to break the status quo to gain adoption.

To highlight this tension, JTBD thought leaders Chris Spiek and Bob Moesta created the Four Forces, also known as the Progress Making Forces diagram[49]:

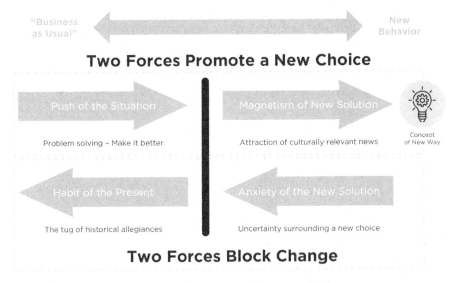

Figure 11.1 – The Progress Making Forces Diagram

Although the differentiated value doesn't actually need to be 10x more, the value must be compelling enough to get prospects to consider. Ultimately, pre-sales in the next chapter will help you understand if the value is enough to get prospects to engage.

Looking at the data, rate from one to ten:

1. **The Job fit**: *Which markets had the exact Job to be Done that your product helps with? Which did Jobs that were very similar?* As mentioned before, if the market doesn't do the Job, then you're simply wasting your time by keeping them in contention.
2. **The unmet needs**: *How much value would be delivered? What would be the impact? Would it be a 10x type of return or just a slight improvement? How likely is it that you deliver 10x? Who would most benefit? Can this be demonstrated?*
3. **Alignment to the budget and problem owners**: If you spoke to other stakeholders, *did they feel the same way? How high is this unmet need on*

their list of priorities? Is there a catalyst for change? Was the opportunity already prioritized? How likely is it to be ignored or postponed?

4. **Alignment to your strengths**: *How well do the unmet needs align to your technology or product's strengths? Is this alignment unique? How many other products or solutions would also be able to deliver this value?*

As we mentioned before, budget generally follows priorities. If you're not sure that this is the case, consider adding another criterion to evaluate the ability to access budget.

(Re)Prioritizing Markets & Sub-Segments

We have data, segments, markets, and scores. The easiest thing to do now would be to create some sort of ranking algorithm and let a spreadsheet make our decision.

However, your team will ultimately need to have the motivation to tackle the market that your algorithm selects, and as we discussed earlier, creating numeric inputs doesn't actually make the data statistically valid. So you should review inputs line by line, and stay away from quantitative assessments.

Your decision should be data-informed, but because you may be working in this market for years, you should also make sure that it works for you and your team.

In my consulting days, I worked on the design of a social network for a large mobile provider targeting the South American market. Their analyses had identified a segment of hyper-engaged users that was extracting a lot of value out of their network. Digging in, they discovered that this segment was largely composed of sex workers, a profession that was illegal in most of their markets. Although there was a clear opportunity for them, no engagement numbers would have convinced a large, well-established company to refocus their social network around the needs of sex workers.

Don't remove any markets from contention at this stage. Simply reprioritize them from best to worst using the criteria you have defined.

Although interviewing prospects is a great way to understand motivations and discover behaviors, it can be dangerous to project the behaviors learned in one-on-one conversations to broader groups of prospects.

At this point, it's a good idea to make sure that the patterns that you identified can eventually lead back to the broader market.

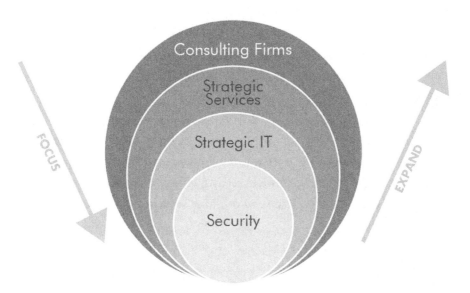

Figure 11.2 – Expanding out of your MVS (Example of Psykler)

Although you may decide to start repositioning your product to win the most promising market on your list (Part V), if you want to avoid challenges like the ones faced by TensorGraph, then you should test the market dynamics before you go all in. We'll see how in the next section.

Case Study :: How TensorGraph Invalidated its Market

Wessam Gad El-Rab founded TensorGraph in 2018. The original goal for the company was to bring to market Enzo, the AI-powered conversational platform that he had created.

Because Enzo was a generalized platform that could address a wide range of customer service problems, it was difficult for Wessam to lock in on the right problem to solve.

The team kept exploring until, through the consulting work that had been funding the company, Wessam discovered that there were more than 20,000 car dealerships in Canada alone. Each of these dealerships had a live chat solution, they had budget, and they were doing a lot of their own support work manually.

This felt like a great fit for Enzo. Not only were there a lot of prospects who understood the value of live chat, their work could be made more effective through service and appointment setting automation, and over time, by learning from the market, Enzo could deliver service quality gains at scale.

Unfortunately, what felt like a great opportunity unraveled when they entered the market and began doing pilot projects with car dealerships.

Dealerships were reluctant to share their historical chat data. Without this data, the initial value of Enzo would need to be cost savings.

By digging in and working with prospects, Wessam realized that their reluctance was hiding something else.

Although Enzo could help dealerships save hundreds of dollars a month, this felt like spare change to companies that were spending hundreds of thousands of dollars a month. Saving $400 a month just wasn't compelling enough for them to switch over.

Although they had the Job, there were problems to solve, and the prospects were familiar with live chat, their value proposition wasn't compelling enough. Businesses don't always care about cost savings; cutting costs wasn't a priority for dealerships.

TensorGraph's foray into the car dealership market was dead in the water. They had lost Enzo's two most compelling benefits, and there didn't seem to be other significant problems that they could pivot to within this market.

Wessam and his team used their learnings to rebrand and refocus their technology to address problems in a new market. The next evolution of their platform, Fluido, is now a no-code platform that helps businesses design, build, and optimize their own conversational AI solutions.

Things often look very different when you have your boots on the ground in a market. Wessam and his team certainly found that to be true.

◀◀

If, like Wessam, you've come to a dead end, consider jumping back to Chapter #6, What Your Product Enables. The analyses therein will help you refocus your enquiry around other value assumptions.

Taking Action (2 hours)

1. Consolidate the information that you collected on each market.
2. Consider narrowing your target(s).
3. Analyze your differentiation, the Job fit, and evaluate the markets

qualitatively.

4. Create a shortlist of the MVS that are still in contention.

IV

Validating Your Findings

In this section, you will run experiments to validate the market opportunities that you identified. Based on the evidence you collect, you'll decide which market to focus on, and which to cast aside.

12

Validating Markets

"Bad ideas you should be able to disprove quickly. Good ideas you should have a ton of trouble disproving. [...] Good ideas are always going to be good ideas and you can't kill them no matter how hard you try. [...] Often, people try to keep alive bad ideas far longer than they should exist.[50]*"* – Lucas Carlson, Serial Entrepreneur

Selecting a market and then wholly dedicating your resources to winning that market is no small feat.

In the same way that you wouldn't just get married after a few dates, you shouldn't put all your hopes and energy into a market without first testing the relationship.

Markets don't always behave exactly the way we expect them to. It's important to confirm that the market opportunities that you're considering can really meet your business goals.

At this point, your most critical risk will be entering a market that you either can't win, or where you can't build a sustainable business.

To cut through a lot of back and forth with prospects, and to validate the opportunity, you need to confirm that they actually want your product. The best way to do this is by asking them to buy.

As we saw in Chapter #2, prospects make purchase decisions based on a mashup of factors—the product benefits, value proposition, brand, social proof, sales experience, features, etc—that all get weighed and evaluated together.

Therefore, to validate the need, you need to make real offers. As *Talking to Humans* author Giff Constable says: *"People don't honestly think about willingness to pay unless they feel like it is a real transaction."*

Preselling is therefore the best way to see if your value/market assumption is truly compelling.

Preselling Your Solution

To make preselling work, it's important to focus on a single use case for a single customer profile.

Prospects in your MVS should be willing to buy to achieve similar results and get the same Job done. You'll have a hard time building a standardized product unless you can get traction on a clear value proposition and a clear product concept.

While you can use landing pages, with payment forms, to presell smaller dollar-value products, even in B2C, it's highly recommended to presell face-to-face, or over the phone. Doing so allows you to capture objections and get direct feedback from the market.

As ConvertKit co-founder Nathan Barry says[51]: *"When you ask someone to buy, they're socially obligated to give you a reason."*

If you already have a product, or a prototype that can deliver the value of your solution, use it. If you don't currently have a product, create a brochure, a one-pager, or a short presentation. Focus on the Job, the needs and the desired outcomes, the problems, the core value, and what makes your product different. The important thing is to establish compelling value, ask for the sale, and commit to a delivery timeline.

Don't worry about how much you charge. At this point, it's more about money changing hands than the actual amount of revenue that you can generate.

You can test multiple markets in parallel if you have enough bandwidth. However, where markets are very different, this may prove very costly in terms of time and distraction.

Go see qualified prospects in your MVS, explain how your product addresses their needs, and listen carefully to understand if they perceive a benefit that is distinct from the alternatives at their disposal.

If they don't buy, make sure you understand why:

- **Was the price too high?** The perception of value was either too low to warrant the change, or the risk and effort was viewed as too high.
- **Were the budgets already assigned?** *Is this a stalling technique? What's the real issue? Could budgets be reassigned?*
- **Is it not a priority?** *Why isn't it a priority? What is getting prioritized over this?*
- **Is there too much risk?** *How can you mold your solution to make it easier to adopt? Can you take on some of that risk?*
- **Will someone object?** *Who? What are their concerns?*
- **Is something missing?** *What features are missing? What outcomes are neglected? Why do these features matter?*
- **Was the value not clear enough?** *Was it the pitch or the value proposition?*
- **Did the proposition not sell enough value?** *What were the expectations? What*

would be deemed as 'sufficient value'? Is the value believable?

- **Was it not the right time?** *Why is it not the right time? Are they lacking resources? Are there ways to reduce the perception of risk?*
- **Are there other solutions in the pipeline?** *What solutions are getting prioritized? Is your product sufficiently differentiated?*
- **Are they committed with the competition?** *How could you create more value or differentiation?*

You'll eventually be able to overcome most of the objections that come up. At this stage, however, you should focus on understanding if prospects in your MVS (those that perform the Job):

1. understand your product's differentiation;
2. perceive it as a valuable improvement over their current solution; *and*
3. find the offer compelling enough to at least consider making a purchase.

Take note of the objections. You'll need to address them later on if you decide to enter the market.

Only consider taking a market out of contention if you tried to close 20 qualified prospects, and none of them understood or perceived the value of your differentiation.

If no one bought, make sure you know why. *Could those reasons be overcome in the short-term?*

Generally, you should close five to ten presales before deciding to commit to a market.

◀◀

> If prospects aren't seeing the value of your product, and you're unable to get presales, consider validating a different market. Alternatively, consider jumping back to Chapter #11, Analyzing Your Findings to prioritize new opportunities.

Testing Market Dynamics

Depending on the type of product that you're working on, you may decide to run other types of experiments to expand your understanding of the market dynamics.

These experiments may include:

- **Testing the Acquisition Process**: If your core goals include signups or engagement, as was the case for Unitychain (next case study), you may also wish to test the acquisition process. Not only will this force you to clarify your value proposition, it will push you to find ways to reach prospects. Acquisition tests will help you flag significant issues with the market and your messaging.
- **Testing the Value and Retention**: If your product depends on hitting certain thresholds of retention or engagement, it can be a good idea to validate whether users are able to get the value they seek, or whether their usage meets the parameters of your business model.

We'll cover both types of experiments throughout the rest of this chapter.

Testing the Acquisition Process

There are two challenges that need to be overcome before you can start testing the acquisition process:

1. You need to find a way to reach *the exact* problem owners that you're trying to sell to; *and*
2. You need enough volume consistently to be able to get conclusive evidence, fast.

Because of these challenges, and the risk of opening Pandora's box by trying to do too much, there are only two channels that can really work at this moment:

- **Cold emails**: unsolicited emails sent to prospects without prior contact; *and*
- **Search and social ads**: targeted prospecting ads through Twitter, Facebook, Instagram, or LinkedIn, or search ads via Google Ads.

Whether you decide to use cold emails, social ads, or search ads, your goal will be the same: you need to test your targeting, your value proposition, and your landing page copy.

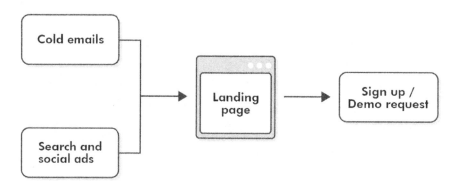

Figure 12.1 – The key steps of a simple acquisition flow

If prospects can freely sign up to your product, you can use sign ups as the core goal for your evaluation. If a demo is required, you can use demo requests or actual demos given as the key action to optimize against.

Based on all the information that you have collected about the prospects and the problem owners in the market, create campaigns that build on your innovation's core value (Chapter #6), and speak to these prospects' needs.

Turn your product benefits into landing page copy, select the appropriate keywords and targeting (for ads), and start testing.

Look at the profiles of people signing up or requesting demos. Improve your targeting until you're able to attract the right prospects, and can consistently get clickthrough rates over:

- 3% for search ads[52];
- 0.90% for social ads[53];
- 5% for cold emails[54].

Those are low-end benchmarks for ads and cold email campaigns.

Once you are able to attract prospects and they're starting to sign up, consider tracking them further down your funnel to understand if they are actually buying and sticking around. This will help you gain deep insights into the full customer lifecycle.

Your goal with testing the acquisition process is to understand whether your messaging *piques* the interest of your prospects. *This*, in turn, will help you learn how your product fits in the market.

By further engaging with these users, or doing demos with them, you'll be able to learn about the gaps they perceive, their objections, the benefits that resonate with them, and the peculiarities of the market.

Don't change your product, or the core value that you're selling. Focus on learning how the value of your product performs on the market first.

Testing the Value and Retention

There's often a chasm between the value that a company sells and the value that customers realize with the product.

To understand this gap and avoid unexpected issues that can hurt your ability to grow and scale in the market, it makes sense to go through the full lifecycle of usage with a subset of prospects or customers.

For example, if you are still evaluating multiple markets, you can bring in five to seven customers per market, deliver the service, and evaluate the gaps while closely monitoring their use and experience.

This will allow you to gather information about:

- **The value discovery**: How well the product matches expectations, how customers make sense of the product, and what struggles they have early on.
- **The support**: When and why they require assistance, how much assistance they require, and whether or not this level of proximity can fit your business model.
- **The usage and engagement**: How the product is used and the value consumed, how consumption evolves over time (does it grow or decline?), and why customers become disengaged;
- **The value realized**: *What value is realized within the first week, the first month, or the first year? How does that value compare to what was being sold or advertised?*
- **The gaps**: *What gaps remain in the product, its onboarding, or its support? How big are those gaps, and how do they affect mid- to long-term value and engagement?*

To start learning, create pilot groups for each of the MVS that you are evaluating. Be very clear about which users or customers are in and out of your pilot studies. Monitor these users closely, while making sure that they're getting the exact same product and services that you hope to deliver to this market.

Let the relationships play out over a few payment or usage cycles (one to three months). Make qualitative assessments at regular intervals.

Compare their experience with the experience of other customers from the same market, and other markets. Don't make changes to your product until you have made a commitment to the market (Chapter #13). Take note of gaps and red flags. *How big is the gap? Could this gap be overcome?*

The information that you're gathering will help you understand the value received. This, in turn, will help you improve the experience should you decide to focus on this market.

Analyzing the Results

Unless you have made adjustments to your messaging to reflect your MVS, the experiments that you have run will probably give you a first glimpse into the challenges of entering a market with messaging that isn't in line with the market.

This should provide opportunities to learn, identify issues, and see the impact on performance. Should you decide to enter one of the markets that you have explored, you'll eventually need to overcome these challenges.

What have your experiments revealed? Have you identified significant blockers? Any issues that can't be addressed? Are there sub-segments worth focusing on?

If you have been able to identify distinct attributes or behaviors that seem to influence how much value prospects perceive in your solution, consider further narrowing your MVS.

Don't remove markets from contention. Re-prioritize markets based on the data points that you acquired. We'll make decisions in the next chapter.

Case Study :: How Unitychain Validated Social Use Cases

Unitychain is a venture studio, but it's also a new blockchain-like structure designed by the studio's founding team.

Realizing that blockchain technology was still a long way from mass adoption, and that the core value of a new protocol like Unitychain would ultimately come from its applications, the founding team decided early on to focus on demonstrating value.

To show how secure and scalable Unitychain was, the team built, or collaborated on the creation of, an ecosystem of products that covered a wide range of use cases—from central bank digital issuance currencies to voting to fintech.

With the aim of further broadening that scope, the team made the decision to enter the social space. Not only could a social network generate a high throughput of transactions, it could also help introduce their technology to new audiences. There was just one issue: they didn't know *what kind* of platform to create.

To get a sense of the opportunities, they joined over 500 Facebook groups across a wide range of topics, looking for high-engagement communities.

By going through group after group, and researching prospects one at a time, the founders realized that educators and content creators were often some of the most engaged participants in communities.

When considering the explosion of online learning, the rise of multimedia content, and the insights that they had captured through their deep dive, there seemed to be an opportunity to create a social product for content creators.

The product that they imagined, *Trail It*, would allow content creators to create interactive walkthroughs and newsletters to engage their audiences. The more *trails* that were created, the more data would pass through Unitychain.

Instead of building the product, the team decided to create a waiting list. As they engaged with creators based on their social media presence, they would track which creators signed up to the waiting list.

The more they learnt, the more effective their messaging became. Soon thereafter, they began reaching out to some of the creators that had signed up, hoping to schedule follow up calls.

By tracking the percentage of creators who were scheduling calls, they iterated, further improving their funnel, and letting creators *self-select* into their beta program.

Step by step, they weeded out the least motivated creators. From then on, they were able to work closely with a small group of content creators and educators to create the product that best matched their needs.

Taking Action (1 to 3 months)

1. Decide if you want to test one, or several markets in parallel.
2. For each market, presell your product trying to close a minimum of five customers.
3. If the acquisition, retention, or engagement of your product has the potential to invalidate your market opportunity, run experiments to test these aspects of the relationship.
4. Assess the results in depth before moving forward.

13

Selecting Your Core Market

"Only choose a market if it makes your strengths obvious." – April Dunford, Obviously Awesome Author

By now, if you've been going through the process in this book, and conducting most, if not all of the analyses, you may be starting to feel restless, itching to start focusing on a market, and growing your business.

If the tests you ran in Chapter #12 confirmed your value/market assumptions, then the decision is an easy one. If, however, the tests showed different promise, or worse, invalidated the markets that you were considering, then you may need to take one step back in order to take two steps forward.

Revisit the prioritization you created in Chapter #11. *Have some of the opportunities begun to look less appealing? Are there some that now look more promising?*

Based on all the research, analyses, and tests you have run, you should be in a position to begin making important business decisions.

Let's get started.

Selecting a Core Market

Your core market is the MVS that you commit to winning.

If things go well, you will focus your team and your positioning on that market and your business will start growing. And by continuously iterating and improving, within a few years, you'll end up owning the lion's share of the market.

For now, you're trying to make the best-informed decision possible. Committing to a market means aligning your product to meet market needs, building trust and credibility with prospects, and finding proactive growth strategies to land customers. These steps will be covered in full in the next section.

So, based on everything you learned, which market:

- *executes the Job that your product enables?*
- *values your product's key differentiators?*
- *is aligned to your strengths?*
- *has budget?*
- *can be reached?*
- *can be sold to?*
- *is a fit for you and your team?*

Let's decide to make that market your core market, and keep going.

Why You Need More Than One Market

By this point, you've done a lot of research (tests, customer interviews, etc)—it wouldn't make sense to just discard the information that you collected.

Because situations change, market dynamics change, and as a result, business strategies sometimes need to evolve, you should track two other types of market opportunities:

1. **A backup option**: In spite of all the tests and research you did, it's impossible to guarantee that the market conditions won't take a turn for the worse. If there were other markets that showed promise, consider making one of them a *backup*. In ideal terms, a backup would be an alternate path that doesn't share any of the major risks of your core market. For example, your backup and core market shouldn't both be affected by the same recession. Should you ever need to make a change, having a good backup option will allow you to pivot, knowing that this market has the potential to make your business a success.

2. **Expansion markets**: If you have found other markets that felt promising, but for some reason are not ideal right now—whether it's because your product lacks functionalities or because there are issues with the market dynamics—it's worthwhile to continue to track them as expansion opportunities. Later on, when you're ready to expand, the data that you have collected will help you make better expansion decisions. Once you're ready, download the extra chapter on expanding your market at findyourmarket.co/expand.

While at this point you might not be left with a lot of great options for backup and expansion markets, it's still a good idea to keep these two categories in mind. The more you develop your core market, the more you'll probably run into opportunities that might fit into one, or both of these groups.

Being responsive to the market—and able to adapt your strategy when a change is required—is a critically important part of building a business.

Cataloging Extra Markets

The challenge with any learnings or decisions made today is that market conditions will change.

Economic changes, or decisions you make, may mean that certain markets become better fits, or they may invalidate them entirely. To be able to quickly revisit your assessments, be as thorough as possible with your note-taking.

For each market that you chose not to pursue today, note:

- the reason(s) why you were initially considering this market;
- discoveries you made through interviews and discussions;
- discoveries you made through tests and experiments;
- the reason(s) why you ultimately decided to choose a different market; *and*
- what gaps or issues, if any, you identified in this market.

You can create a spreadsheet to track these markets. Alternatively, you can download our template at findyourmarket.co/roadmap to get started fast.

Consider revisiting this list quarterly, or even more frequently if needed. Although you want to fully commit to your core market, it's always a good idea to keep track of other opportunities, and to update your assessments the more you learn about the landscape.

Why Committing is Hard

Limiting the size of the market that you're targeting can seem counterintuitive. You started with a grand vision. You know how big your business can be. Focusing on a small market or a MVS feels boring; it takes you away from the epic vision.

By focusing on one segment, you're excluding desirable customers that your product could help.

As entrepreneur Nathan Barry says[55]: *"Choosing a niche is the easiest advice to give and the hardest advice to take. When you don't have traction, it feels like choosing a niche will exclude the few people who are coming in the door."*

However, in research published in the book *Predictably Irrational*, author Dan Ariely demonstrated that when people are given multiple paths to potential success, they try to retain all paths open as long as possible. They do so, even when selecting a specific path would guarantee more success.

If you have investors, or if you're looking for investment, you'll inevitably feel that they want you to *think bigger* or *widen your market*.

To invest, they will want to see potential revenues of more than $100M in a market worth $10 billion or more, just so they know that your company can reach a valuation of a billion dollars.

It's hard for them to extrapolate growth from a *smallish* entry market into a large market. They might think that your idea is too small, or that your business isn't worth their time.

You might hear:

- *"You're thinking too small"*, or
- *"Your market isn't big enough"*, or
- *"It might make sense at Series A or B, but not early on..."*, or
- *"We only fund **ambitious entrepreneurs** who want to **change the world**"*.

Steer clear of outside pressures. Your objective is to build a successful business, first. As Wealthfront co-founder Andy Rachleff says[56]: *"A niche market is the key to the mass market."*

Early on, the benefits of leverage and focus far outweigh the challenge of grappling with what is often a more competitive field of players chasing a bigger opportunity.

When you move from selling to everyone to selling to a well-defined market, it can feel as though you're facing a tremendous loss of potential.

But, when we make the decision to sell to everyone because we're too scared to sell to just a few people, we end up wasting resources, branding our company as generic, neglecting efficiency, losing out to competitors, and failing.

With a clear target, you get to market, sell, and create tremendous value from limited resources. *This*, in turn, helps you make better decisions.

Your expansion and backup opportunities could still be there when your company is ready to expand, or *perhaps* new and better opportunities will have emerged along the way. By that point, you'll be in a better position to expand and win new market opportunities.

Don't fear committing to your core market. Once you have locked in on a great opportunity, you need to go all in.

From this point on, you should start tightening your PMF. This process of iteration is covered in depth in my book, *Solving Product*.

Case Study :: How the Market Found UiPath Six Years In

UiPath was founded as a software outsourcing company called DeskOver, by Daniel Dines in Romania in 2005.

In the early days, the company was bootstrapping, using the revenue from its outsourcing and consulting work to fund the development of its own products.

Their first product took too long to ship, it was late to market, and when it did launch and clients proved unwilling to pay for it, they didn't kill it fast enough.

Although they learned and they kept building, things took a turn for the worse in 2011 when the company lost its biggest outsourcing client[57].

The company's future was in doubt. Instead of folding up, they decided to cut costs and double down on the automation libraries and SDKs that they had been building.

It wasn't clear what the specific use cases were, but the eureka moment came when a customer, the Indian chapter of a large business process outsourcing (BPO) company, showed Dines how they had been using the toolkits. This chapter was at the forefront of the nascent robotic process automation (RPA) market. They were using UiPath's toolkits to train software to mimic tasks like data entry for banks.

Wanting to learn more, Dines sent three of his best people to the customer site in India. What they brought back would change the company's trajectory.

Dines explains[58]: *"We understood there was a huge market out there of people who just do repetitive processes all day long, for whom our technology, which emulates what people do, is perfect."*

In 2012, UiPath launched its first product specifically targeting the RPA market. Within the year, they signed partnerships with global business process outsourcing and consulting firms. By the time 2013 came around, the company was growing fast.

Over the next few years, UiPath grew alongside the market. The need for process automation was being amplified by aging populations and overworked staff.

In 2017, RPA truly emerged as a new enterprise software category, proving itself in terms of ROI and business outcomes, and in 2018, UiPath became the first unicorn in Romania.

Through perseverance, and a fair bit of luck, UiPath found a booming market. When the opportunity came knocking, they were able to commit and do the work needed to take over the market. It took UiPath 13 years to get from $0 to $1M ARR, but from the moment the market picked up it only took them 18 months to reach $100M in annualized revenue[59].

Taking Action (2 hours)

1. Analyze all data points. Use the best information at your disposal to select a core market, and a backup option. Take note of any promising expansion opportunities.
2. Write down your reasoning and your assessment of each market.
3. Commit to winning your core market.

V

Speed

In this last major section, you'll learn how to adapt your positioning and go-to-market strategy in order to gain a foothold in your market and grow.

14

Committing to Your Market

"At a startup, someone inevitably has to become the Chief Focus Officer.[60]*"* – Hiten Shah, Serial Entrepreneur

Once you've made the decision to focus on a market, you need to wholly commit to it.

No, it doesn't mean that you need to let go, or to start neglecting the customers that fall outside of your core market. But, moving forward, your team needs to focus the bulk of its efforts and energy on winning your main market.

There are a lot of things to do. These challenges won't waste your team's entire resources and attention.

In this section, we'll cover:

1. how to create commitment in your organization;
2. how to position your company on the market; *and*
3. how to start proactively landing more of the *right* customers.

Let's start at the top, making changes to your internal priorities.

Committing Internally

One of the most important things in a startup is the decision-making process.

When it's clear internally who your product is for, suddenly the scope of discussions narrows, better decisions get made more quickly and with fewer debates, and your team is able to spend more time solving customer problems.

To reach this level of clarity, the founders and the management team first need to agree on the type of customers that the company is focused on.

When everyone is able to tell the difference between a good and a bad lead, why that difference matters, what the consequences of targeting the wrong leads are, and how long your company intends to keep this focus, then your entire organization gains clarity.

Everyone, from back-end developers to outside sales staff, needs to commit to the same go-to-market strategy. To make sure that this focus is shared across your organization, consider adjusting your employees' bonus structures and evaluation criteria so that they reflect the new targeting.

If you don't commit internally, staff will be forced to debate and argue each time a promising lead from another market reaches out. Ultimately, it's through commitment that your team can achieve great velocity.

Swedish data visualization startup Spotfire (now part of TIBCO) is a company that used this type of strategy to great effect.

Although Spotfire began as a generalized solution targeting a broad range of markets, their early successes in pharma and biotech, with customers like Astra and Unilever, convinced them to focus wholly on the chemistry, biology, and pharma markets.

From the moment that decision was made, the company's president and COO, Rock Gnatovich, told teams to stop taking calls from prospects from other markets. Such strength of commitment led to accelerated growth.

Eventually, when the company had gained a dominant share of its core market, Spotfire's leadership was able to revisit messages that prospects had left, to identify their next market opportunity.

You need speed to create momentum, but you won't be able to create speed if your team isn't 100 percent committed to winning its market.

Address this challenge first. Once your team is fully committed, and it knows exactly what it's trying to achieve, you can begin making an external commitment to your market.

Committing Externally

Up until now, your messaging, your marketing, and your distribution strategy haven't been aimed at any specific market or segment. Now, every aspect of your company's external image will need to be adjusted to reflect your new market positioning.

Your value proposition needs to change from *'look at all the great things that can happen with our product'* to *'here are the specific problems that we can solve for customers just like you'*.

All touch points must tell this same story. Moving forward, your website, your ads, your sales collaterals, your landing pages, your whitepapers, your testimonies, your social media accounts, your client lists, your product and customer success messaging, and your case studies *all* need to be adapted to your market.

As author and entrepreneur Tim Ferriss says in *The 4-Hour Workweek*: *"People can dislike you [...] but they should never misunderstand you."*

You'll only get one shot at positioning per prospect. Very quickly, you'll need to make sure that your messaging communicates:

1. who you help;
2. how you help; *and*
3. what's so great about the way you do it.

Your messaging will become more impactful once it's aimed at an audience. Not only will this help you to attract and convert the right leads, it will also help drive recommendations and word of mouth, which in turn will attract even more customers.

In the coming pages we'll look at the various elements of your external positioning that will need to be adapted, but to be able to make these changes, you first need to know *what* to put forward...

Case Study :: How Wistia Discovered How it Could Reach its Customers

Wistia was founded by Chris Savage and Brendan Schwartz in 2006.

Although the company now offers a video marketing platform, their story didn't start that way.

In their first year, the founders built a platform to help artists create their own portfolio sites[61]. However, this platform proved difficult to monetize, and they decided to refocus on the video component that they had created.

They tried to sell it to compliance departments inside organizations, the medical device industry, and prospects in telecommunications—before eventually realizing that their video features resonated most with marketers.

Running in so many directions and only locking in on their fifth target meant that they hadn't had the time to understand marketers in depth. This was something that became abundantly clear the day they started discussing marketing strategy with Ron, one of their early customers[62].

The founders wanted to get his take on their marketing plans. Their idea was to write blog posts that they would share on Reddit and Hacker News.

Ron's reaction stunned them. He had never heard of the sites that they were hoping to target. Instead, during his commute, Ron read industry publications and newspapers like *The Boston Globe*. He spent literally none of his time in the places where the founders were hoping to promote Wistia.

The more they learned about marketers, the more they realized that they had no idea where they spent their time. They needed to figure out what books they read, what content they consumed, and what movies they were watching in order to be able to reach them.

Through various tests and discussions with customers, the founders eventually found the right blogs, channels, and communities to target. Things became much clearer once they made marketers their decision-makers, and they did the hard work of figuring out where they spent their time.

Deepening Your Understanding of the Market

As Profit Well founder and CEO Patrick Campbell says[63]: *"If you don't do segment and persona analysis, you better be able to raise a ton of money. I guarantee you there's some persona or segment on some vision document or in that euphoric part of your entrepreneurial brain that is completely wrong for your business."*

To avoid missing the mark in the way Wistia did, you need to understand where your prospects spend time, how they look for solutions like yours, how they compare them, what aspects of products they value, who they look up to, and how their objections can be overcome.

If you've been doing interviews with prospects throughout this book, you probably already have a lot of the information you'll need. You may already know:

- where prospects look for advice;
- what platform(s) they use to exchange ideas with other members of the market;
- where they research and compare solutions like yours;
- where they spend their time;
- what podcasts they listen to;
- what films and videos they watch;
- what social media platforms they use;
- what events and conferences they go to;
- what live events they attend;
- who has influence over them;
- who they listen to;
- what language they use when they're looking for products like yours;
- how they frame the value they seek;
- what benefits they want;
- what price points they consider;
- what tradeoffs they're willing to make;
- how they like to buy; and
- what generally prevents them from buying.

If you do, consider skipping over this section to start making improvements.

The clearer your answers are, and the more in tune you are with the actual people that you are targeting (with all their nuances), then the better your marketing will be.

If you're still unclear about some of the answers, consider doing a new round of interviews with recent users and customers in your market. To gain a broader perspective, consider also including qualified prospects that didn't buy, or sign up.

Now that you're committed to winning this market, it makes sense to dive even deeper. The information captured during these interviews will be useful for many purposes.

You can get started by asking questions like the following:

- *How would you describe your role as [Role]?*
- *What does success look like for you?*
- *How did you first hear about [Product]? What did you know about it at the time?*
- *What was going on in your life at that time?*
- *Did you imagine what life would be like with the product? What were you expecting?*
- *What was your previous experience with [Solution Space]?*
- *What made you decide to [Buy / Use] the product?*
- *Did anyone else weigh in on the decision?*
- *Did you evaluate other products? Which ones?*
- *Once you [Signed up / Bought], how did the product compare to your expectations?*
- *Did you feel you had all the information you needed to get started?*
- *What was the main thing that convinced you?*
- *Did anything make you hesitate in buying [Product]?*
- *Now that you have [Product] what can you do that you couldn't do before?*
- *What is the main value you feel you've received from the product?*
- *What is the main problem you feel the product solves for you?*
- *What does success look like when using [Product]?*
- *Why do you keep using the product?*
- *Now that you're using [Product], who would you recommend it to and why?*

- *How does [Product] work with other related products or services you currently use?*

You'll want to spend a lot of time learning about the catalyst—what was going on in their company when they began thinking about looking for a solution like yours (e.g. a new funding round, a new leader joining the company, etc). You want to understand causality—what events made them decide to move forward, and what held them back.

By focusing on the way that they shopped and *hired* your solution, you'll be able to learn about what builds or reduces trust, the alternatives, how prospects compare solutions, and what gets them over the finish line.

Dig deep into their decision-making process. Ask open-ended questions and follow their emotions to capture stories.

Consider recording the discussions. The words and phrases that they use, especially around their needs, problems, and benefits, will help you to craft effective messaging. In the end, your interviewees' words could prove to be even more valuable than the information they shared.

Aligning Touch Points

To properly target your market, you must craft your website, product messaging, and touch point communications in a way that attracts the attention of your problem owners.

Your communications should reflect their language and their worldviews, should be crafted in a way that helps bring them along their solution journey.

You should put a special emphasis on:

- **The touch points**: *On what platforms are you visible? What tactics are you* *using to catch the attention of your problem owners? How are you bringing problem owners along?*

- **The benefits and the value propositions**: *What core value are you promoting? What benefits support your value proposition? What pain points do you refer to?* Be specific. As Tony Ulwick says in his book *What Customers Want*: *"Precision, not vagueness, is the key to communicating a product's true value."*
- **The tone, the style, and the language**: The tone and language you use will need to be different depending on whether you're targeting established CEOs, or 20-year-old marketers. Your language should reflect the way your prospects speak.
- **The images and the visuals**: The images and visuals should fit your problem owner's worldview, education, gender, race, etc—but you should consider making them as inclusive as possible.
- **The content**: Your content should speak to the reality of the problem owners in your MVS. It should help educate them on the solution space, and help them address related problems.

Don't worry too much about *over-committing* to your market. As serial entrepreneur Amy Hoy says: *"If you aren't repelling people, you're not attracting people either."* It should be very easy for your problem owners to know whether your product is for them.

As you make changes, monitor the types of prospects that are being attracted by your messaging. Keep making changes until you are able to attract the right people.

Your external positioning will need to evolve and be refined over time. Expect to keep making refinements the more you learn about your market.

You can download a checklist at findyourmarket.co/checklist to make sure that you're not neglecting any of your key touch points.

While this is all a great start, it's probably not enough. Prospects will also want to know that other people like themselves are able to find success with your solution.

Aligning References

Case studies are an essential currency in B2B. They can allow businesses to quickly establish credibility, and create separation over the competition.

The important thing with case studies is that they reflect the worldview of your prospects. Problem owners must be able to see themselves in the references you use.

Case studies are usually best worked into contract renewals (not new contracts), because when you first sell a deal, you can't know for sure that the product will work for the customer.

A great case study allows your prospects to really get to know the customer. Case studies need to:

1. explain the problem;
2. introduce the referring company/product and their situation;
3. describe how their challenge was overcome; *and*
4. sum things up—give the story a happy ending.

Case studies need to include real numbers, they need to talk about specific strategies that were actually used, and they need to quote customers in their own words. All this will make these stories feel more relatable.

If you're not sure where to start when creating case studies, you can use our guide at findyourmarket.co/case-studies.

Unfortunately, not all your customers will be willing to let you produce case studies.

Some clients may be limited in what they can say or share publicly. Others might simply not want to. If that's the case, consider asking them instead to use their company name and logo on your website, write a short testimonial, publish a joint press release about the deal, write a blog post or technical paper about the experience, or jointly present at a conference.

There are many ways to get creative with references. Make sure that prospects are able to see themselves in the examples and references that you use on your site and in your collaterals. This will help them to imagine the success that your product could deliver for them and their organization.

Getting Embedded in the Market

Once you've aligned your touch points, and your references are able to attract the right customers, you'll want to take things a step further.

To get even deeper in the market, you should establish relationships with domain experts. These could be:

- **Influencers**: People with their own influence, or who are working for influential companies in the market. You can generally find the experts by looking at the content that gets frequently shared in the market. *What names often come up? Which organizations often get mentioned or quoted?* Alternatively, you can look at the roster of speakers and panelists at important events and conferences, frequent guests of podcasts, and endorsements that get repeated in the market. All these should point you to influencers. Don't simply look for people who are influential in general, focus on market influencers.
- **Experts and salespeople selling or working in the industry**: There are probably people who are already selling to your prospects, or who are working in some other capacities on servicing those customers. These

people already know what is *sellable*, they know the levers and the pain points, and they also have connections. They can teach you a lot about the market. Eventually, they'll be the people that you want to hire, or those that you'll want to ask to find the right people to hire.

- **Other companies selling in the space**: You may be the first with a certain type of solution in this market, but there are probably other organizations serving other needs in the market. Get close to those organizations and their founding teams or CEOs. They can help open doors, provide insights that can be difficult to get, or even team up with you on deals.

By establishing a presence at watering holes, you'll increase the odds that you run into important domain experts, and you'll learn what matters. Look for the watering holes by asking yourself where customers congregate, or where they gather for pleasure and for work. Those could be conferences, tradeshows, restaurants, bars, hotels, professional association networking events, or any other type of online communities.

The more embedded you become in the market, the more the market will pull you towards the things that matter most to it. This is exactly what happened to the founders of Flutura.

Case Study :: How Flutura Embedded Itself in the Oil & Gas Market

Flutura was founded by Derick Jose, Krishnan Raman, and Srikanth Muralidhara in 2012.

Early on, the founders were seduced by deep learning and The *Industrial* Internet of Things (IIoT). The combination of their interests led to the creation of Cerebra, their first AI platform.

At that stage, it wasn't clear what problems Cerebra could solve. What was clear, however, was that they weren't headed in the right direction.

Thankfully, when they realized that their platform could ingest high-velocity electro-mechanical sensor streams, they were able to course correct. *This,* they hypothesized, could be very valuable to the energy industry.

But although the founders had a wealth of business experience, and had worked together for years, none of them had direct experience in the energy industry. They would need to go deep in order to understand whether or not their product could help oil and gas organizations.

To begin learning, they immersed themselves in Houston, the *Silicon Valley* of the energy industry, casting a wide net, and hoping to discover as many problems as possible.

Through half-day Lunch and learns, time spent with retired Industrial/Oil and gas executives, and networking events, they were able to gain deep insights, and identify many problems that Cerebra would be able to solve.

Derick Jose explains: *"We did a lot of Thursday evening drink and learn sessions. This was a big hit. We gleaned insights which probably would not have been expressed in a formal controlled setting."*

The more they learned, the more they realized that the energy industry valued two key attributes in product offerings: reliability, and real dollars saved.

Their analyses allowed them to lock in on the key problems that Cerebra could solve, and by using the network that they had built up in the sector, they landed their first three orders. By that point, they knew that they had found the right opportunity.

Today, Flutura has hundreds of customers in the oil and gas, heavy machinery, and process manufacturing industries. As Flutura can attest, going deep in your target market can really pay off.

Becoming a Key Contributor

Once you've entered the market, you need to quickly transition into a thought leadership position.

Not only will this allow you to get even deeper in the market, it will attract prospects, and increase your company's credibility. When customers recognize your company as an expert, they are more likely to want to buy from you, and to refer your product[64].

Get to know the players in the space. Spend time with them. Show that you care, and that you're building for the long run. If you are serious about winning your market, then you need to be part of the community.

Start by organizing events and get-togethers, moderating online communities, curating content for the market, or promoting the work of influencers.

Add value. Be visible. Once you're beginning to build expertise or have gathered unique information, share it widely. You can present at conferences, create video content, or produce thought leadership content (articles, whitepapers, research, etc).

The deeper your company gets in the market, the more opportunities will open up. Consider organizing a conference, creating free tools to help the market at large, getting involved in professional associations, writing a book, or making company resources available to different players in the market.

The transition from new entrant to active vendor to key contributor will help cement your company's position as a pillar of the market. This is ultimately the transition that you're trying to make.

Taking Action (4 weeks)

1. Meet with your co-founders and your management team. Crystallize who your product is for, and who it isn't for. Make sure everyone in your company is clear about that distinction.
2. Revisit the interviews that you did in your core market and the customer interactions that you had. If you're not sure about what prospects are looking for, or how you should speak to them, interview 15–20 users or customers to find out.
3. Align your company's touch points, tone, style, language, images, benefits, value proposition, social media, and content strategy to the needs of your market.
4. Create market-specific case studies and testimonies. Start building references.
5. Look for ways to speed up market understanding and increasing your visibility.
6. Become a thought leader. Start making contributions in your market.

15

Proactively Growing Your Customer Base

"Audience building should really just be called "earning trust at scale.""
– Alex Hillman, The Tiny MBA Author

Imagine this. After committing to your market, your company goes through a complete rebrand. You use some of the value propositions learned and iterated through interactions with prospects, but nothing changes in terms of your acquisition strategy. *How long do you think it will take for your company to get 10% of the market? 20%? 30%?*

If you have PMF, you'll probably still gain market share through referrals, a bit of luck, and organic channels. Chances are, however, that it will take a lot longer than you'd like. In reality, if you don't move fast and scale, someone will beat you to it. To win, you need to maximize speed to ubiquity in your market.

In a good market, customers reference each other when making purchase decisions, and word of mouth helps amplify the growth efforts. But for this type of fire to spread, there needs to be a flame.

To accelerate growth and own your market, you need to invest time and resources in speeding up discovery.

If you just keep doing what you've been doing—or if you simply rely on customers finding you—you'll have a hard time reaching the required velocity to capture large shares of your market.

This is why, to grow fast and to grow predictably, you need proactive growth.

When you seek out and target the exact folks that your company exists to serve, then you can focus your resources on leads that convert, you can grow more systematically, and you will avoid being pulled in different directions.

Proactive Growth Strategies

Although you *could* start by doing the things that don't scale[65]—capturing visibility on communities, blogs, forums, or speaking at targeted events—soon you'll realize that these tactics are more hit and miss than you want.

Sometimes these tactics will be able to bring in a lot of prospects, and sometimes they won't. The channels you should quickly transition to are those that:

1. allow you to **directly** reach problem owners; *and*
2. can be scaled.

On the surface, it might seem like there are thousands of ways to acquire users and customers. But in reality, there are just a few channels that will yield results quickly:

1. **Search Engine Marketing**: Promoting your product via ads on search engines like Bing or Google can help you reach prospects when they're actively looking for a solution.
2. **Social and Display Ads**: Advertising on Facebook, Twitter, Instagram,

or LinkedIn can also help you reach the right prospects quickly.

3. **Outbound Sales**: Contacting prospects by phone or via email can help you build your initial pipeline, and ensure you have a constant stream of conversations with problem owners.

4. **Distribution/Resellers**: *Could you tap into another organization's distribution channels? Could their salesforce help get your product in front of customers?* Sometimes marketplaces (e.g. Salesforce, Shopify, Slack, Atlassian, etc) can work. Sometimes another organization can act as a reseller. These channels can be worth exploring.

Although you can use any of these channels to get started, down the road, the unit economics of your business will limit your choice:

- **Your CLV (Customer Lifetime Value)**: This is the predicted amount that a customer will spend on your product throughout the entire relationship. CLV is expressed as a dollar amount, and is usually calculated by multiplying the average revenue per customer by the average length of the customer relationship. For example, if customers pay you $100 per month on average and they usually remain customers for 22 months, your CLV would be $2,200.
- **Your CAC (Cost of Acquisition)**: This is the average cost of winning a customer for your product. The CAC is also expressed as a dollar amount, and can be calculated by dividing all the costs spent on acquiring customers by the number of customers acquired in the period that the money was spent.

Because you always want your CLV to be at least three times as much as your CAC, you might eventually realize, for example, that using outbound to sell a product that only costs a thousand dollars a year isn't really profitable.

Ultimately, you need to run tests to find a channel that will work for your unique product/market combination. Focus on testing one acquisition channel at a time. Run rapid experiments to look for signs that you're heading in the right direction.

Keep experimenting until you find a channel that works. When you find one, put all your efforts into acquiring as many customers as possible from that channel.

Once a channel is working, word of mouth will amplify your growth, thus creating a flywheel[66] that will help further accelerate your growth.

Proactive growth leads to velocity, but even proactive growth strategies can be amplified...

Creating an Echo Chamber

Proactive growth strategies help to create the momentum that referrals and word of mouth then help to amplify on the market.

Now, if your flywheel is working, you will grow and start winning market shares.

To further tighten your grip on the market, you can put time and effort into creating an echo chamber effect, to ensure that every time prospects look for a solution in your product category, they see your brand. This is a strategy that email marketing software provider ConvertKit (next case study) executed to perfection.

To get started, go back to what you learned during the interviews in Chapter #14. By breaking down the information collected in these interviews, you'll be able to understand actual customer journeys. Focus on understanding:

- where prospects exchange information;
- where they go to talk about products like yours;
- where they start their search when they look for solutions;

- what keywords they use when searching; and
- how they share information.

Your goal will be to make sure that your product is visible on all sites, channels, and platforms along your prospects' journey. When well executed, this approach will help to amplify your messaging and build awareness.

Consider:

- **Forums and communities**: Look for the informal communities of your prospects— online watering holes like forums or self-hosted communities where they might have already been discussing your product.
- **Quora**: Quora is part forum, part social network. Its users might already be asking questions about your product, be seeking advice, or be looking for help with their purchase decisions.
- **Groups**: LinkedIn and Facebook groups are great ways to find expressed needs. Look for related keywords to understand where prospects are exchanging on topics that relate to your business.
- **Blog posts/Resources**: Look for the resources and blog posts that show up in the search results for the keywords that prospects are using. *Can you help contribute to these resources? Could you add helpful comments? Could you find a way to get a link back to your site?*
- **YouTube**: YouTube is the home of *How-to* videos. The same general ideas can apply there.
- **Reddit**: Many prospects are probably also looking for solutions or advice on Reddit. You might find great discussions there. There might be other interesting conversations on Product Hunt, Hacker News, GrowthHackers, etc.
- **Slack communities.** There are thousands of Slack groups that congregate around roles, industries, or topics of interest. Discovery platforms like Slofile[67], or curated lists like Standuply's[68] can help you find the best Slack communities to target.
- **Servers and channels**: Different communities will use different platforms

to engage. There are also many groups connecting on Discord and Telegram. DISBOARD[69] has a public list of Discord servers while the aptly named telegramchannels.me[70] centralizes 18,000 Telegram channels.

- **Twitter**: People share things on Twitter that they often wouldn't share on LinkedIn or Facebook. Consider following relevant keywords and engaging.
- **Product reviews**: Platforms like G2, Capterra or TrustPilot help buyers find the products that best match their needs. *Could you improve your visibility and positioning on these platforms?*
- **Events and conferences**: *What real world or virtual events do your prospects attend? Could you gain visibility at these events? Could you find a way to reach your prospects by targeting events and conferences?*

You can use tools like AnswerThePublic[71] to find relevant groups, questions, and discussions, or SparkToro[72] to find sites, podcasts, and influencers to target. Consider taking note of the links and resources that prospects are sharing—this will help you discover even more sites along the journey.

Consider also asking new users and customers:

How did you discover [Product]?

Reverse customer acquisitions. *How did your best customers find you? Could you gain visibility along **their** journey?*

The more visibility your company gains in your target market, the more your messaging and positioning will get amplified. Create a journey that helps convert referrals and casual searchers into buyers.

Case Study :: How ConvertKit Created Echo Chambers Through Micro Niche Targeting

ConvertKit was founded by Nathan Barry and David Wheeler in 2013.

In its first year of operation, the company struggled to carve a niche in the competitive email marketing market; few people had heard of them, they were barely making money, and it was difficult to land customers.

The founders had experience using content marketing to sell products, but for ConvertKit, this approach wasn't working.

During that first year, the founders never considered doing outbound—it wasn't something they knew, and in some ways, it felt *icky*. However, 20 months in, it was time to try something new.

Through direct sales, they could create highly targeted lists of prospects. They would then contact these prospects to learn about their issues setting up their email marketing programs, and eventually, getting them to switch to ConvertKit.

Initially, they spent a lot of time trying to understand who was already finding success with their product. Their goal was to turn these users into case studies that would help convince their peers.

Instead of directly targeting professional bloggers—the high-level market that they were targeting—they drew very small circles, and went after micro niches.

By targeting, for example, 40–50 bloggers at a time in a niche like *professional men's fashion bloggers in NYC*, they were able to tap into existing relationships between bloggers.

As the bloggers began migrating to ConvertKit, they felt like *everyone on the Internet* was switching to ConvertKit when, in reality, it was the micro niche and their close networks creating that effect. Through narrow targeting, tiny echo chambers were created, and these were being amplified by their sales efforts.

Although ConvertKit couldn't make outbound sales profitable when accounts only cost $50–75 per month, this strategy helped to kickstart their growth.

The more sales they closed, the more word of mouth built up, and the more word of mouth built up, the faster they grew.

Nathan explains[73]: *"Word of mouth is the best way to grow a company, but you need traction for the referrals to start. That's where direct sales come in. By choosing a niche, listing our prospects, and getting in touch directly we no longer had to wait for them to come to us."*

By positioning themselves as "email marketing for professional bloggers" and then going after niches within this market, ConvertKit began to grow. Their targeting made the messaging clearer, the roadmap thinner, and the prospect lists basically wrote themselves.

Nathan kept doing outbound for another two years while they built out their inbound capabilities and an affiliate program that, today, drives 30% of their sales[74]. Their approach helped build a company that now generates more than $25M in annual sales[75]. Although their targeting has since expanded, ConvertKit is still a lot more focused than many of its competitors.

Taking Action (∞)

1. Use your learnings to come up with a proactive customer acquisition strategy.
2. Conduct experiments to find the right distribution channel for your product.
3. Seek to create an echo chamber effect around your prospects.

VI

Conclusion

16

Conclusion

"The key to success is to hang around long enough to get lucky.[76]*"* –
Carl Quintanilla, American Journalist

Sometimes it takes years for the true value of an innovation to materialize...

Enter Andrew Weinreich, who in 1997 founded SixDegrees, the first social
network to allow users to create a profile, show their friends list, and search
through friends based on the concept of Six degrees of separation[77].

SixDegrees was a moderate success at the time, attracting 3.5 million members, and at the height of the Dot-com bubble the company was acquired by
YouthStream Media Networks for $125 million.

Although at face value this could be viewed as a great success, what makes
this story particularly interesting is that, early in the company's lifetime,
Weinreich patented the idea of the social network.

Within the next few years, YouthStream Media would follow SixDegrees to
the grave, and Weinreich's patent[78] would hit the market, becoming one of
the hottest assets at auctions.

The full value of the patent may not have been clear to its previous owners, but innovators like Reid Hoffman (LinkedIn) and Mark Pincus (Tribe.net, later Zynga) quickly understood its potential.

In 2003, the pair acquired the patent for $700,000, beating out 20 other bidders including *then* media giant, Yahoo!

The concepts Weinreich had dreamt up just six years prior were to become part of the foundations of LinkedIn (acquired by Microsoft for $26 billion), Tribe.net (now defunct), and Facebook (in which Hoffman had invested, now worth well over $800 billion).

Although Weinreich ultimately explained away SixDegrees' failure as having hit the market too early[79], it's hard not to wonder what might have happened had he held on to his intellectual property.

There's *Almost* Always a Positioning

This is an extreme example, meant to show what *can* happen to an innovation. As a founder, it's important to always be aware of the value that you've created.

As long as you have proof that what you have built, or are building, is valuable, and you're able to fund your business without putting yourself at risk, it makes sense to keep going.

Over the years, what I've learned about startups is that a large part of succeeding is being able to iterate and keep pushing.

It's simple. The faster you learn, the faster you can iterate. The faster you can iterate, the faster you can find a winning market opportunity.

By looking at the various companies covered in this book, we can see that:

- It took two years for Informavores (Chapter #3) to finally find a good market. *What if they had given up before?*
- It took Jive (Troubleshooting) five years and several pivots to find the right model. *What if they had given up before?*
- It took UiPath (Chapter #13) six years to find the core value of their technology. *What if they had given up before?*

These are examples of winning startups—but for every winner there are many more products and innovations that fail.

At this moment, there may be no way for you to know whether you're sitting on a winning hand or not, but it's my hope that the models and concepts covered in this book will allow you to make the right decisions, and know when to pivot, persevere, or cut your losses.

Parting Words

You've made it through *Find Your Market.* To make it to your business goal, however, you will need to stay humble and keep moving.

This may read like fortune cookie wisdom, but it truly is the key.

Plan for iteration, don't expect things to work the first time around, and leave enough room to implement your learnings.

The best game plan for this requires humility, resilience, and a good eye for knowing when to course correct.

Under *Troubleshooting,* you'll find vignettes that have been designed to help you recognize, and ultimately overcome, moments of struggle.

When in doubt—or if I haven't answered a specific question that you had—I invite you to search through the hundreds of articles available on the companion website (findyourmarket.co/blog), or to get in touch with me directly at etienne@findyourmarket.co.

Thanks for reading *Find Your Market*.

-Étienne

If you feel inclined to help us out, the best way is by posting a review on Amazon, sending us feedback or suggestions, or recommending Find Your Market to friends or other founders.

VII

Troubleshooting

In Troubleshooting, you will find content to help you recognize when your business is due for a change of strategy.

17

How to Know if You're Spinning Your Wheels

"The thing about inventing is you have to be both stubborn and flexible. The hard part is figuring out when to be which." – Jeff Bezos, Amazon Founder

Business projections made early in the life of businesses rarely work out.

In part, this is because projections fail to consider that the early days of new ventures tend to be research and development (R&D), and that sadly, R&D projects don't always work out.

Basing any projections on the certainty of discovering critical business answers within a set timeframe is ludicrous at best.

Innovation success can't be guaranteed. Neither can timelines. This is the reason why VC firms only expect one out of ten startups to be truly transformational, and expect the other nine to either fail or merely return their original investments[80].

In innovation, it's necessary to budget enough time and money to be able to explore markets and validate opportunities. But it's also important to be able to let go of bad ideas, when they're showing signs of being bad.

That said, it's not because you *can't* do precise planning that you shouldn't try to minimize your risk.

Although The Lean Startup and customer development are great tools for helping to manage a startup's risk, they don't provide signals that tell innovators and entrepreneurs *when* to course correct.

Without these signals, timelines can stretch, innovators can lose their way, and the wheels can start spinning.

In this section, we look at some of the telltale signs that can indicate that a business has begun spinning its wheels and should, perhaps, consider a change of strategy.

Should you feel the need to use this content, it will help you lock in on the exact stage that you find yourself in, and help you carve your best path forward.

1. Trying to Scale a Non-Market

Initially, or even later on, you may find that it's very challenging to get prospects to try your product or to want to engage. The ratio between site visitors, ad impressions, or reachouts and actual conversions may be abysmal. It can be difficult to find platforms or channels that consistently allow you to find new customers.

Because you're trying to speak to the needs of multiple audiences, and you haven't adapted your messaging to a specific market, prospects may not recognize themselves in your sales and marketing messaging. And even if they do see the value of your product, they may not be willing to recommend it to others, because it's not clear who it's for.

Signs

Few customer referrals. Customers with vastly different needs and profiles. Difficulty seeing patterns when interacting with customers. Low clickthrough rates on ads (<0.5%) and outbound communications (<3%). Low conversion rate (<1%).

Solution

Go through the analyses in Chapters #3 and #4. Adjust your positioning and communications to speak to the needs of your best market segment (Part V). Track customer referrals, looking at the roles and profiles of the customers that come in through referrals. Make sure there is consistency in your acquisition model, and that you're able to learn from the right folks. Attempting to scale a business while straddling several markets is a costly strategy.

2. Trying to Sell a Product That Lacks Differentiation

You're selling in a market—or multiple markets—but lots of deals fall through. When customers buy, they don't seem particularly thrilled or engaged. Customer churn is high. Product abandonment is high. Customers often try to negotiate or to get special deals when they buy. The product doesn't feel very compelling.

Selling a product that's undifferentiated—or that has differentiation that's not particularly valued by your prospects or customers—reduces your ne-gotiating power, and also customers' willingness to buy and their desire to engage. Your product may be perceived as a commodity, and that perception can be hard to change. You'll have a hard time growing a product that's undifferentiated.

Signs

Low pricing power. Customers feel emboldened to ask for discounts. High churn. Customers switching between vendors. Customers that don't really seem excited to hear about your product's key differentiators.

Solution

Differentiation is not just about being different, it's about being different in a way that customers feel is *better*. Engage with customers—yours and the competition's—to understand what value they seek, as seen in Chapter #6. *Could you make your product 10x better along a dimension that a sub-segment of the market values? Could you address more Jobs or switch to a more important customer Job?* If you don't feel like any of this is possible, or if you feel your product's differentiation *should* be valued, consider looking for new markets, the way we did in *Part III*.

3. Key Strengths Neglected

You have entered a market, positioned your product to meet demand, and are beginning to acquire customers—but it seems like the customers you're landing don't value what you and your team feel is so unique about your technology.

Customers may be sticking around, maybe even recommending your product, but what they value and what they ask for in terms of new features doesn't line up with your business strategy. *Do you go with the flow, or is it time to make a change?*

Signs

Core differentiators under-utilized. Feature requests that don't line up with your business strategy. Customer feedback that contradicts your understanding of your product's core value.

Solution

If what customers value in your product is something that can ultimately help create a sustainable competitive advantage, then you may have stumbled on a new, unanticipated, opportunity. Once you have defined that value (Chapter #3), it may make sense to decide to shift your focus and strategy to take on that opportunity the way Vimeo did in the next case study. However, if the value isn't long-term, or if it feels like a weaker strategic fit for your product, it might make sense to sustain the product *as is* while you prioritize product development based on the needs of a different market.

*Are there sub-segments of customers that value your product for the **right** reasons? What are the differences in their profiles?* Find out using the analyses from Chapters #3 and #4. It may ultimately make sense to reposition your product to address the needs of this MVS.

Case Study :: How Vimeo Shifted From Being a YouTube Alternative to a $5B B2B Company

Vimeo was created by Zach Klein and Jake Lodwick, the founders of College-Humor, a comedy video site, in 2004. At the time, the founders wanted an extra site to share and tag short videos[81], which they were hoping to grow as a sideline.

CollegeHumor's success, with more than 6M visitors per month, had begun attracting attention—enough that in 2006, IAC, a large holding company, decided to acquire the whole company.

When reviewing the assets they had purchased, IAC discovered Vimeo, a platform that they felt could compete with YouTube (which had recently been acquired by Google at high price).

Wanting to take on the established players and to differentiate Vimeo from the competition, IAC directed the co-founders to expand the site's functionalities.

Vimeo kept growing, relying heavily on innovations like creating better upload tools, better curation of content, and high-definition content.

But no matter how fast Vimeo grew, it couldn't completely escape YouTube's shadow. To keep gaining market share, Vimeo kept innovating, considering major pivots into streaming services[82], before eventually figuring out what product they had been building all along...

Vimeo CEO, Anjali Sud, explains[83]: *"What I saw, I think where we eventually went, is everyone was focused on the viewer experience over the content, but what about all the people that had to make that content?"*

Many of the features that they had built—like high-definition video formats, editing tools, and live-streaming functionalities—had opened up new opportunities for them. The company was now perfectly positioned to capture a large share of the $20 billion market for video hosting, distribution, and monetization. They could continue to be a YouTube alternative, or they could pivot.

In 2017, Vimeo put it all together, repositioning itself as a SaaS platform offering a suite of tools for video creators. The company was now addressing bigger pains, and they had the perfect product to take on that opportunity.

Today, with more than 1.6 million paying subscribers generating over $200M in revenue, Vimeo has reached new heights. Through multiple pivots and reinventions, the company found its way to profitability and a valuation well over $6 billion.

To reach your goals, sometimes you need to be willing to reinvent yourself, even when it means changing something that's already successful.

4. Multiple Good Markets

After going through the various analyses in this book, you may be left with a few opportunities that seem about equal. There are good reasons to go after each of these opportunities, and it's hard to pick just one. If you select one, the other ones may not be available later. *What should you do?*

It's hard to know what *might* happen if you go after either of the opportunities. There has to be a way to pick the best one.

Signs

Indecision. Long wait time before deciding to position your product to take on a market. Debates. Arguments. Fear of alienating business partners or employees. No clear path forward.

Solution

Analysis paralysis is real. It might not feel like it, but delaying market selection might hurt your business down the road when your run rate is limited. It's time to make a decision. Select the opportunity that can be won the fastest, whether it's the market you're most familiar with, or the one in which prospects buy more rapidly. Keep the other opportunities as backups (Chapter #13). Although they may not still be options when comes time to expand, the opportunity cost of staying still is much greater. Time to make a decision!

5. No Ideal Market

You've gone through the entire process in this book, and have perhaps even been through the cycle a few times. In spite of all this, you're still looking for a great market for your innovation. Time is running out. *Does this mean game over?*

If you're still unable to get customers after three months trying to sell (Chapter #12) in the most promising markets that you identified, then you may be at a crossroad. It may be faster for you to start from the market—trying to understand customer problems and needs—than to try to get your existing innovation adopted. Sadly, this happens.

Signs

Unable to get pre-sales. Qualified prospects don't seem interested. Difficulty getting air time with prospects. Value proposition doesn't feel very compelling.

Solution

There is no *perfect* market. *Could you at least get pre-sales in one market?* Pick the most promising markets and focus on selling: *Do prospects with the actual Job consistently dismiss your product? Why? Could your team overcome their objections in the near-term?*

If it doesn't feel likely that you'll start winning deals within the next three months, then you may need to accept that your technology simply isn't perceived as *valuable.* Start from a customer need. You may be better off building new innovations from scratch based on market demand. *What would you need to do to win prospects' business? Could you do this within a reasonable time frame?* If you decide to pivot, make sure you can get pre-sales (Chapter #12) before you write another line of code.

6. The Market Just Can't Meet Your Goals

You have found a market, you've reached PMF, and your company is growing—but the more you learn about the market, the less it feels like it will allow you to reach your goals. Whether it's because of its size, competitive dynamics, the level of service required to close deals, or any other reason, your business may be working, but ultimately it feels like a dead-end.

This is exactly the situation Jive (next Case Study) found itself in. You may have the right product, but be in the wrong market. Or perhaps, it's the reverse. Breaking something that works to go after a new opportunity feels like a massive gamble. *Is this just shiny object syndrome*[84], *or is your assessment justified?*

Signs

Trends or projections are not headed in the right direction. The business is turning into something you didn't want it to be. It feels like you're missing out on bigger and better opportunities.

Solution

Don't kill a successful business. Use it to fund experimentation the way Jive did. Allocate time and budget into finding a new market (Part III), or a new product opportunity. As much as possible, try to view this as an extension of what you're currently doing, not a reboot. The transition will be faster if you can reuse some of your existing assets.

Case Study :: How Building Three Different Products Helped Jive Find the *Right* Market Fit

Jive was founded by technical co-founders Bill Lynch and Matt Tucker in 2001. Because neither founder wanted to be CEO, they quickly brought on Dave Hersh, a management consultant, to lead the business efforts.

Although their goal was to create a large company that could go public, raising capital wasn't really an option in 2001. The Dot-com bubble and the uncertainty caused by the 9/11 terror attacks had made investors reluctant to invest.

Despite this setback, Jive's first product, collaboration middleware, was a success. Customers were buying, they were happy with the solution, and within a few years, the company had managed to pass $15M in sales.

Although the founding team was happy with the success, the product wasn't "right". Collaboration middleware wasn't strategic enough—it wouldn't allow them take the company public.

With clients to serve and no short-term needs for outside capital, the team began experimenting with new products.

Over the next few years, they pursued an opportunity selling to support departments, which proved too small, and an opportunity selling real-time communication tools, which brought them in direct competition with behemoths like Cisco and Microsoft. But in 2006, as enterprises were starting to adopt Wikis and Web 2.0 tools, they found their fit.

It was about time. Their customers—the companies that were funding their experimentation—had begun to grumble. There were bugs and issues that they wanted to see solved, but by this point, the company was all in on its new collaboration software.

Letting go of more than $15M in sales was a major gamble, but they had already made early sales for their collaboration software, and had already seen traction from large enterprises—and collaboration middleware just wouldn't allow them to go public.

It took Jive five years to find PMF for an opportunity that matched their ambitions. If they had raised capital early on, they probably wouldn't have been able to pivot this often, or this drastically.

They had to find the right opportunity before they could hit the gas pedal. Once they did, they raised $15M from Sequoia Capital, and they were off to the races.

In hindsight, Hersh says[85]: *"I think there's a lot of entrepreneurs who get impatient for growth and want to get there really quickly, and as a result take shortcuts that I think ultimately can bring the business down. [...] Take time, find the right path **before** plugging a bunch of money and energy into something that you think is the right one."*

In 2011, Jive went public raising $161 million from investors, and in 2017, the company was acquired in full by Aurea Software.

Patience paid off in spades for the founders. Sometimes it makes sense to take a step back so that you can take two steps forward.

7. Your Market Expansion Doesn't Add Many Distinct Customers

You've come full circle. You have been able to build a sustainable business in a good market. You have captured a large enough market share that you can start thinking about expanding in new markets. However, the market you have chosen to expand in isn't bringing in nearly as many new customers as you expected. The growth you had anticipated now seems unlikely. *What to do?*

Signs

Your focus has expanded, but your growth rate hasn't increased. The new customers that you're landing were already aware of your product. The profiles of your new customers feel very similar to those of your initial customers. There isn't a lot of engagement on your website's market-specific sections or case studies.

Solution

Dig deeper in your market sizing. *Are the new prospects that you're targeting also part of your original market?* Markets that are too closely related run the risk of overlapping. It's likely that eventually you would have landed these customers, without making changes to your strategy. Improve your targeting. Explore new market expansion opportunities. Take bigger risks. Go after markets that are more distinct, with less relatedness.

Next Steps

Thanks for reading *Find Your Market*.

Unfortunately, reading is one thing, applying is another.

To help you apply the ideas in this book and find the right market for your innovation, I have put together a series of templates (invitation emails, interview scripts, etc), worksheets, and calculators.

You can download these resources at: **findyourmarket.co/bonus**

Need Help With the Methodology?

Growing a business is hard. Unfortunately, even with the best techniques, case studies, and a full book to refer to, you may still have questions.

Maybe the situation you find yourself in is atypical, maybe there are different techniques that could be appropriate, or maybe you'd like to discuss the approach in greater detail.

No matter the reason, I understand quite well that some situations require going *off script*.

Each month, I help several innovators, founders, and product teams work through their specific challenges.

If you feel I can help, connect with me at **findyourmarket.co/coaching**. It will be my pleasure to help you work through your specific challenges.

Acknowledgments

Find Your Market would not have been possible without the generous contributions of the following growth experts and entrepreneurs: Alex Berman, David Waroquiers, Derick Jose, Jon Jones, Joshua D. Tobkin, Kingsly Kwalar, Melike Bozkaya, Miles Tabibian, Patrick Vlaskovits, Tom C. Wren, and Wessam Gad El-Rab.

Other people who have played a key role in the writing of *Find Your Market*—reading through drafts, giving suggestions, providing feedback—include Étienne Thouin, Joy Sellen, Prasad Chalasani, Sébastien Bibeau, and Simon Vosgueritchian.

A big thanks must also go out to the various authors, researchers and entrepreneurs mentioned in this book. From Aaron Levie to April Dunford and Amy Hoy, their work helped fuel and inspire the writing of *Find Your Market*.

Thanks for helping to make this book a reality.

References & Further Reading

To dive deeper into the concepts in this book, I recommend reading:

- *Crossing the Chasm*, Geoffrey A. Moore
- *Demand-Side Sales 101*, Bob Moesta
- *Founding Sales*, Peter R Kazanjy
- *Lean B2B*, Étienne Garbugli
- *Lean Customer Development*, Cindy Alvarez

- *Obviously Awesome*, April Dunford
- *Running Lean*, Ash Maurya
- *The Four Steps to the Epiphany*, Steve Blank
- *The Jobs To Be Done Playbook*, Jim Kalbach
- *The Lean Startup*, Eric Ries
- *The Mom Test*, Rob Fitzpatrick
- *Traction*, Gabriel Weinberg and Justin Mares
- *Where to Play*, Marc Gruber and Sharon Tal
- *Working Capital*, Sean K. Murphy

Notes

WHY THIS BOOK

1 **Expand your addressable market to drive your next wave of growth**
https://www.intercom.com/blog/how-to-expand-your-addressable-market

2 **The Top 20 Reasons Startups Fail**
https://www.cbinsights.com/research/startup-failure-reasons-top

3 **Why Start-ups Fail**
https://hbr.org/2021/05/why-start-ups-fail

4 **ConceptShare**
https://www.crunchbase.com/organization/conceptshare

ProofHQ
https://www.crunchbase.com/organization/proofhq

ReviewStudio
https://www.crunchbase.com/organization/reviewstudio

5 **Best Employee Engagement Software**
https://www.g2.com/categories/employee-engagement

6 **Highlights**
https://www.gethighlights.co

7 Google Analytics, Outlier.ai, etc.

THE STARTING POINT

8 https://twitter.com/dtrinh/status/1346211709141340160

9 An often-cited example of this is the release of Facebook's News Feed in 2006, which was met with a lot of criticism causing some users to boycott the company. Over time, the feature was adopted and became a major contributor to Facebook's revenue.
https://en.wikipedia.org/wiki/News_Feed

10 **10 Startup Sales Tips from Dreamforce 2015**
https://davidcummings.org/2015/09/16/10-startup-sales-tips-from-dreamforce-2015

MINING FOR GOLD

11 **How Intercom Co-founder Des Traynor Uses "Clusters of Demand" to Find Product-**

Market Fit
https://underscore.vc/blog/how-intercom-found-product-market-fit/

12 **How to prioritize features using NPS®**
https://www.atlassian.com/agile/product-management/how-to-prioritize-features-usi
ng-net-promoter-scores

13 **Building a company and selling it to Salesforce.com**
https://www.linkedin.com/pulse/20141205233842-662991-building-a-company-and-se
lling-it-to-salesforce-com/

CAN IT BE A MARKET?

14 **Reedsy**
https://reedsy.com

15 **The Hive Index**
https://thehiveindex.com

16 **Look Before You Leap: Market Opportunity Identification in Emerging Technology Firms**
https://www.researchgate.net/publication/37463914_Look_Before_You_Leap_Market_
Opportunity_Identification_in_Emerging_Technology_Firms

WHAT A GREAT MARKET LOOKS LIKE

17 **Veeva Systems: A Brief History**
https://www.fool.com/investing/2017/03/29/veeva-systems-a-brief-history.aspx

18 **Veeva defied detractors when it launched a cloud life sciences biz a decade ago**
https://techcrunch.com/2017/02/25/veeva-defied-detractors-when-it-launched-a-clou
d-life-sciences-biz-a-decade-ago

19 **Salesforce, Inc Revenue 2006-2020 | CRM**
https://www.macrotrends.net/stocks/charts/CRM/salesforce,-inc/revenue

20 **Veeva: The Biggest Vertical SaaS Success Story of All Time**
https://www.saastr.com/veeva-biggest-vertical-saas-success-story-time-video-transcr
ipt/

21 **Average cost of developing a new drug could be up to $1.5 billion less than pharmaceutical
industry claims**
https://www.lshtm.ac.uk/newsevents/news/2020/average-cost-developing-new-drug-c
ould-be-15-billion-less-pharmaceutical

22 **Gaëtan Gachet: "How Algolia Scaled up to $10MM ARR & Beyond"**
https://youtu.be/1GiJCp6x1UE?t=1114

23 **The Sharp Startup: When PayPal Found Product-Market Fit**
https://medium.com/craft-ventures/the-sharp-startup-when-paypal-found-product-
market-fit-5ba47ad35d0b

24 The Serviceable Available Market (SAM): The part of the market that can actually be won

when accounting for the competition, geographic and cultural constraints, regulations, financial limitations, willingness to pay, market cannibalization, etc.

25 Serviceable Obtainable Market: The market share that they believe that they can currently win.

26 **Turning Products Into Companies**
https://underscore.vc/guidebook/turning-products-into-companies

WHAT YOUR PRODUCT ENABLES

27 Note: You could also argue that the Job to be Done is the manager's goal of showing progress for the marketing team.

28 *"Consumers overvalue the existing benefits of an entrenched product by a factor of three, while developers overvalue the new benefits of their innovation by a factor of three. The result is a mismatch of nine to one, or 9x, between what innovators think consumers desire and what consumers really want."* – John T. Gourville, Economist

Eager Sellers and Stony Buyers: Understanding the Psychology of New-Product Adoption
https://hbr.org/2006/06/eager-sellers-and-stony-buyers-understanding-the-psychology-of-new-product-adoption

29 *"Consumers overvalue the existing benefits of an entrenched product by a factor of three, while developers overvalue the new benefits of their innovation by a factor of three. The result is a mismatch of nine to one, or 9x, between what innovators think consumers desire and what consumers really want."* – Dr. John T. Gourville

Eager Sellers and Stony Buyers: Understanding the Psychology of New-Product Adoption
https://hbr.org/2006/06/eager-sellers-and-stony-buyers-understanding-the-psychology-of-new-product-adoption

30 To test your Job statement, *The Jobs To Be Done Playbook* author Jim Kalbach suggests answering:

- *Does the statement reflect the Job performer's perspective?*
- *Does the Job statement begin with a verb?*
- *Is there a clear beginning and end point to the Job?*
- *Might the Job performer think, "The [Object] is [Verb]-ed"? (e.g., did the financial portfolio grow? Or was food sold on the street?);*
- *Would people have phrased the JTBD like this 50 years ago?*

31 Personal opinions.

32 **Jobs to Be Done: Theory to Practice**
https://jobs-to-be-done-book.com

33 **What Type of Lean Startup Experiment Should I Run?**https://medium.com/@Kromatic/what-type-of-lean-startup-experiment-should-i-run-3360d89596fe

34 **Growth Hacking and Startup Ideas with Patrick Vlaskovits**
https://www.craftsmanfounder.com/growth-hacking-and-startup-ideas-with-patrick-vlaskovits

35 **Superpowered Co-Founder Patrick Vlaskovits on the Importance of Focus and Anti-Personas in B2B**
https://findyourmarket.co/vlaskovits

VALUE/MARKET ASSUMPTIONS

36 https://twitter.com/levie/status/1371645834496864258

37 **Escaping the Prior Knowledge Corridor: What Shapes the Number and Variety of Market Opportunities Identified Before Market Entry of Technology Start-ups?**
https://www.researchgate.net/publication/259889205_Escaping_the_Prior_Knowledge_Corridor_What_Shapes_the_Number_and_Variety_of_Market_Opportunities_Identified_Before_Market_Entry_of_Technology_Start-ups

38 **Data.europa.eu**
https://data.europa.eu/euodp/en/home

Data.gov
https://www.data.gov

Data.gov.uk
https://data.gov.uk

PRIORITIZING MARKET ASSUMPTIONS

39 **To Diversify or Not To Diversify**
https://hbr.org/1997/11/to-diversify-or-not-to-diversify

40 https://twitter.com/petergyang/status/1333088921903763456

41 **Something Old, Something New: A Longitudinal Study of Search Behavior and New Product Introduction**
https://www.researchgate.net/publication/228581182_Something_Old_Something_New_A_Longitudinal_Study_of_Search_Behavior_and_New_Product_Introduction

42 **How to Create a Customer Development Panel**
https://findyourmarket.co/panel

43 **Gaëtan Gachet: "How Algolia Scaled up to $10MM ARR & Beyond"**
https://www.youtube.com/watch?v=1GiJCp6x1UE

44 **Algolia Raises $110 Series C To Improve Search Functions**
https://news.crunchbase.com/news/algolia-raises-110-series-c-to-improve-search-functions

FINDING THE BUYERS

45 **The Challenger Sale**
https://www.gartner.com/en/sales-service/insights/challenger-sale

46 **26th Edition: February 2021**
https://cmosurvey.org/results

ANALYZING YOUR FINDINGS

47 **9 Things First-Time Founders Get Wrong About the Journey**
https://www.linkedin.com/pulse/9-things-first-time-founders-get-wrong-journey-jas
on-m-lemkin

48 **Your Product Needs to be 10x Better than the Competition to Win. Here's Why:**
https://bothsidesofthetable.com/your-product-needs-to-be-10x-better-than-the-com
petition-to-win-here-s-why-6168bab60de7

49 **Unpacking the Progress Making Forces Diagram**
https://jobstobedone.org/radio/unpacking-the-progress-making-forces-diagram

VALIDATING MARKETS

50 **#5 Lean Guru, Patrick Vlaskovits**
https://www.youtube.com/watch?v=4UWG3fd3DYg

51 **SPI 244: Bootstrapping a Startup with Nathan Barry from ConvertKit**
https://www.smartpassiveincome.com/download/Transcript-SPI244.pdf

52 **Google Ads Benchmarks for YOUR Industry**
https://www.wordstream.com/blog/ws/2016/02/29/google-adwords-industry-benchmar
ks

53 **Facebook Ad Benchmarks for YOUR Industry [Data]**
https://www.wordstream.com/blog/ws/2017/02/28/facebook-advertising-benchmarks

54 Assuming an open rate of 30% and one in six people clicking through after opening.

SELECTING YOUR CORE MARKET

55 **15 lessons from our first $15 million**
https://nathanbarry.com/15-lessons-15-million

56 **Startups Always Have a Chasm to Cross**
https://medium.com/@arachleff/startups-always-have-a-chasm-to-cross-61b79215ac
05

57 **From Communism To Coding: How Daniel Dines Of $7 Billion UiPath Became The First Bot Billionaire**
https://www.forbes.com/sites/alexkonrad/2019/09/11/from-communism-to-coding-ho
w—daniel-dines-of-7-billion-uipath-became-the-first-bot-billionaire

58 **The story of UiPath – How did it become Romania's first unicorn?**
https://business-review.eu/news/the-story-of-uipath-how-it-became-romanias-first-
unicorn-164248

59 **Form S-1** https://www.sec.gov/Archives/edgar/data/1734722/000119312521094920/d9855
6ds1.htm

COMMITTING TO YOUR MARKET

60 https://twitter.com/hnshah/status/1369005181849899008

61 **Wistia Cofounder On How To Sell To Businesses**
https://mixergy.com/interviews/savage-wistia-interview

62 **Wistia Cofounder On How To Sell To Businesses**
https://mixergy.com/interviews/savage-wistia-interview

63 **How to price your SaaS product – Issue 49**
https://www.lennysnewsletter.com/p/saas-pricing-strategy

64 **Can Being A Thought Leader Drive Sales?**
https://www.mspinsights.com/doc/can-being-a-thought-leader-drive-sales-0001

PROACTIVELY GROWING YOUR CUSTOMER BASE

65 **Do Things that Don't Scale**
http://paulgraham.com/ds.html

66 **The Flywheel Effect**
https://www.jimcollins.com/concepts/the-flywheel.html

67 **Slofile**
https://slofile.com

68 **2,000 Slack Chat Groups and Communities**
https://standuply.com/slack-chat-groups

69 **DISBOARD**
https://disboard.org/servers

70 **telegramchannels.me**
https://telegramchannels.me

71 **AnswerThePublic**
https://answerthepublic.com

72 **SparkToro**
https://sparktoro.com

73 **15 lessons from our first $15 million**
https://nathanbarry.com/15-lessons-15-million

74 **Personal Journey Of a SaaS Founder with Nathan @ ConvertKit.com - Escape Velocity Show
#8**
https://www.youtube.com/watch?v=v7P8f0msNyw

75 **Control Center – Baremetrics**
https://convertkit.baremetrics.com

CONCLUSION

76 **Carl Quintanilla: Why You Should Say Yes**
https://www.spartanrace.ca/en/community/podcast/episodes?article=30004

77 **Six degrees of separation**
https://en.wikipedia.org/wiki/Six_degrees_of_separation

78 **Patent 6,175,831**
https://patents.google.com/patent/US6175831B1/en

79 **The Facebook Effect**
https://www.simonandschuster.com/books/The-Facebook-Effect/David-Kirkpatrick/978
1439102121

HOW TO KNOW IF YOU'RE SPINNING YOUR WHEELS

80 **The Venture Capital Secret: 3 Out of 4 Start-Ups Fail**
https://www.wsj.com/articles/SB10000872396390443720204578004980476429190

81 **How Vimeo became hipster YouTube**
https://fortune.com/2011/02/23/how-vimeo-became-hipster-youtube

82 **Vimeo CEO on Business Model and Strategy**
https://www.bloomberg.com/news/videos/2017-11-09/vimeo-ceo-on-business-model-
and-strategy-video

83 **How Vimeo Pivoted Away From Original Content and Found its Niche**
https://www.streamingmedia.com/Articles/Editorial/Featured-Articles/How-Vimeo-Piv
oted-Away-From-Original-Content-and-Found-its-Niche-129733.aspx

84 **Shiny object syndrome**
https://en.wikipedia.org/wiki/Shiny_object_syndrome

85 **#4 Jive Founder, Dave Hersh**
https://www.youtube.com/watch?v=tri7PoLUqA8

About the Author

Étienne works at the intersection of tech, product design, and marketing.

He's a three-time startup founder (Highlights, Flagback, and HireVoice), a five-time entrepreneur, and a customer research expert.

In 2014, he published the first edition of Lean B2B: Build Products Businesses Want. The Lean B2B Methodology has helped thousands of entrepreneurs and innovators around the world build successful businesses.

You can connect with me on:

- https://findyourmarket.co
- https://twitter.com/egarbugli
- https://www.facebook.com/leanb2b
- https://www.linkedin.com/company/leanb2b

Subscribe to my newsletter:

- https://findyourmarket.co/newsletter

Also by Étienne Garbugli

Étienne's books focus on leveraging customer insights to build and grow businesses.

Lean B2B: Build Products Businesses Want

https://leanb2b.co/pdf

Lean B2B consolidates the best thinking around Business-to-Business (B2B) customer development to help technology entrepreneurs quickly find traction in the enterprise, leaving as little as possible to luck.

The Lean B2B methodology is used by thousands of entrepreneurs and innovators around the world.

Solving Product

https://solvingproduct.com/pdf

Solving Product offers a simple, unique, and wildly powerful business compass.

It was carefully designed to help product teams and entrepreneurs reveal the gaps in their business models, find new avenues for growth, and systematically overcome their next hurdles by leveraging the greatest resource at their disposal: customers.

Printed in Great Britain
by Amazon